Dear Jean,

Your Great Contribution
Tells Me Much about you.
On Page #172 begins a chapter
of God speaking To you about
The anointing and Calling on
Your life!

God Loves you! I Love you!

Gary Carnahan

THY KINGDOM COME

by
GARY LARRABEE

Published by the International Branch of the Lion of Judah. For book
orders, call 1-800-862-4811 or visit www.pineorchard.com

Color illustrations in center of book are printed by permission of
Revelation Productions. Artwork © 1982, 1992 Pat Marvenko Smith.
www.revelationillustrated.com 1-800-327-7330

Printed in Canada.

ISBN 0-9700644-0-3

We walk by faith, not by sight.

— *2 Corinthians 5 : 7*

Contents

PART III

Table of Charts

Table of Illustrations

Statement of Appreciation

I want to state my appreciation to the many ministries, individuals, and Bible teachers that the Lord has used to bless me or give me a clearer understanding in some area of His Word.

Years ago, as I listened to Kenneth Haggen speak about the corporate anointing, the Holy Spirit revealed that the Branch spoken of in Isaiah 11:1-5 was not a single person, but the body of Christ in unity, all of one mind and accord, spoken of as one person.

Similarly, as I listened to Dr. Gene Scott in 1980, the Holy Spirit confirmed things that I had been told about prophetically: the separation of Judah and Israel and their regathering as one nation again in this generation.

Arthur Blesset stands out in my mind as a role model of total commitment to the Lord.

Trinity Broadcasting has blessed me beyond measure with their many guests: Dwight Thompson, Benny Hinn, Kenneth Copland, and many others.

I especially feel close spiritually to Watchman Nee and the many books he has written that have helped me in becoming the person I want to become, that *Spiritual Man*.

INTRODUCTION

If someone were to tell me the things that I will be telling you as you read this book, I'm not sure even *I* could believe them to be true. The same will most probably be true with you. No one likes to be looked upon as one out of step with reality. Yet it appears to me that I have been made aware of a new reality, that is, a *Spiritual Reality*. If I were to state my opinion, I would say, "Things seem to actually happen first in the Spiritual Realm before they are seen as truth and fact in the physical reality of our lives." But that is an opinion and may or may not be true.

The only thing that *never* changes is absolute truth. It is eternal and lives forever. We simply may not be completely aware of what that truth is. I am seeking truth. But the truth of what I say will only be seen in the reality of future events.

I have stated the truth of the events that have already happened, but the future events that I will speak about are my opinions based upon the knowledge and experiences that I have had. You will see that I have written about what I believe the Lord has spoken to me. If what I have written is not the truth, the error is mine.

However, it is not my intention to deceive. Only to reveal what the Lord wishes me to. My *mind* tells me that a lot of what I write about is unrealistic, but my *heart* and complete faith in the Lord seems to be telling me that it is truth and I must speak it and write about it, regardless of how I feel.

As to whether or not it will be believed, I will leave the results to the Lord. If the Lord is speaking, nothing can keep it from happening. If it is just Gary Larrabee speaking, nothing can be done to make it happen.

PART I

My Story

As I look at life, I see the extremes of both good and evil. I see the defeated and the victorious. I see the sick and the healthy. I see success and failure. It appears that life blesses one and destroys another without reason. Sometimes the one that life blesses ends in failure, and sometimes the one that life tried to destroy ends in success.

The key seems to be a decision of the will to find the purpose of life. The answer lies beyond self. The self is unable to make sense of or find the reason why. No matter how hard one may try, it does not guarantee success. In fact, in many cases the greater the effort, the greater the failure. Try as hard as you can, and success evades those who are here on earth for a special purpose.

The trials and failures of life can almost destroy the entire person. I liken it to being burned alive: some are called to go through a refiner's fire of extreme pain and sorrow. It seems that they are near death emotionally. You come to the point of emotionally dying to all earthly desires and life on this earth. At the point where there is no more determination, there seems to be a jewel of perfection not of ourselves. The jewel is a totally new start in our life's purpose. It is a life of total rest and total peace, regardless of any circumstances.

This life requires that we do not look at our circumstances outwardly. We must cast our total being upon the Lord. We must place life itself on the line of believing that Christ is directing our lives and has brought us to the point that our life depends upon Jesus Christ being in control, regardless of how bad the circumstances. He has a purpose and is leading you through it. Knowing that as each step is made, He will take you on to the next step for His purpose alone.

If this truly describes your life, you must surely not only be called according to God's purpose but *chosen* and *prepared* for God's purposes. Your being used by God does not depend on your talents or your position in life. Rather, it is your disappointments and failures that make you qualified for the job.

Matthew 20:16
16. *So the last shall be first, and the first last: For many be called, but few chosen.*

I will not describe my many failures that brought me to the Lord prior to 1968. I will begin with the failures that brought me to the point of being called by God ten years later.

In the middle of a very hot and trying day, I went home to an empty house. My wife, whom I loved dearly, had left me, and this was one of those hard times back in 1978. I had just gone through my fifth business failure as the owner and broker of a real estate company in Boise, Idaho. The harder I tried, the worse it became. It was as though I was riding a dead horse into the ground.

No matter how difficult it became, I wouldn't quit. I just kept getting deeper and deeper into financial trouble.

I refused to give up hope. I had deals that seemed ready to close but something would always happen. Success was always elusive, just beyond my reach.

God, is that You?

By the twenty-first day of July 1978, I was at the end of my rope. I began praying desperately for a way out of my problems. I was home alone sitting on the couch and was barely conscious of my Bible resting beside a box of Mini-Wheats on the coffee table. I seemed to say in my mind, "God, please speak to me."

I reached instinctively for this Living Bible and read, "In the seventh month and the twenty-first day" *(Haggai 2:1).* I stopped reading. This *was* the twenty-first day of July 1978. *The seventh month and the twenty-first day.*

I began to wonder, *Could God really be speaking to me?* I prayed not to be deceived and said aloud, "God, if You are speaking to me, I must be sure. So I will close the Bible and open it somewhere in the beginning or in the middle or towards the end, but please tell me whether this is Your word of truth for me."

The words I read were: "My word is truth, like wheat is to grain." There may have been more to the sentence, but the word *truth* stood out to me because I asked for truth. Then I noticed the box of cereal sitting of the table. The box of Mini-Wheats. Mini-Wheats are made out of *grain*. This made me believe that something supernatural truly was happening.

I read the whole second chapter of Haggai and the eighteenth and nineteenth verses seemed like ones of pure hope.

Haggai 2:18, 19

18. *Consider now from this day and upward, from the four and
    twentieth day of the ninth month, even from the day that the
    foundation of the Lord's temple was laid, consider it.*

19. *Is the seed in the barn? Yea, as yet the vine, and the fig tree,
    hath not brought forth; from this day will I bless you.*

I believed I was being told that I would receive a
blessing on September 24, 1978.

At that time, I thought the Lord was telling me to step
out on faith, so I went every day to an empty office. I was
determined to see what might happen on the ninth month
and twenty-fourth day according to what the Lord showed
me.

The answer was survival one day at a time. Every day
supposedly woud lead me to a position where I will
someday be given finances that will not only help me, but
I will act as a channel according to the Lord's promise to
help people all over the world financially.

On September 24, 1978, a lady came into my empty
office. I didn't actually know her, although I knew *of* her.
She entered my office and said, "I want to work for you."
This was very strange, strange indeed, so I just listened.
She stated that as she was praying, the Lord told her to
come and work for me. I found it intriguing that she chose
to come see me on the ninth month and the twenty-fourth
day. I hired Beatrice, and we struggled a little longer to
hold onto my business. Nothing happened.

Where were the blessings promised?

A month or so after I hired Beatrice, I moved out of the

office. My home and car had been repossessed and I had no money. Beatrice, naturally, moved on and I was completely destitute. I had no place to live and no transportation.

At one of these desperate points, I ran into Beatrice again. I was attending a Bible study called *The Open Door* at an old building downtown. The first time I went, I saw Beatrice inside, among a small group of people. She explained that she owned the building. She knew of my predicament and offered to let me stay in an empty upstairs apartment until I could get things together for myself. This must have been part of the blessing promised for the ninth month and the twenty-fourth day: the day I met Beatrice.

This Bible study was very different from what I was used to. They raised their hands, praised the Lord openly, and spoke in tongues. I was a little nervous, to say the least, because when I was introduced to the Lord ten years earlier by a good friend, he encouraged me not to associate with people who spoke in tongues.

One of the ladies at this Bible study was a prophetess named Esther. What she spoke was amazing. She stood in front of me and started saying all kinds of things about me. I had never seen her before in my life, but she was saying things that no one else knew besides me. She was saying that I would be used by God to do certain things, and she described some of the things I would be doing in the future.

This became pretty serious to me. If it was God speaking, I'd better pay attention; but if not, I'd better get out quickly. I decided to take a tape recorder and see if I could match everything up with scripture to see if what was being said was true.

I wondered how I got myself into this situation. This was my first experience at seeing people so energized.

I was torn between whether to believe all of this or not. What if God really was trying to communicate with me? This was a decision only I could make. I decided to thoroughly check the scriptures, to test the prophecies according to the scriptures, and wait to see what happened.

I recorded every word spoken prophetically to me at the Bible studies. I then wrote every word down in notebooks, word for word. Then I studied and compared every word with similar events described in the scriptures.

These Bible studies were held several times each week and many of the prophecies seemed to be directed at me. The final conclusion of my study was that the Lord was speaking with the same precepts and personality as the words spoken in the Old Testament by the prophets.

To understand, I compared symbols, themes and concepts, a little bit here and a little bit there. Then the Lord showed me that my approach of searching each prophetic word, though spoken in tongues, was the correct way of discerning these mysteries of God. This was exactly how the Old Testament scriptures of Isaiah say that prophetic words, spoken in tongues, should be interpreted.

Isaiah 28:9, 10
9. *Whom shall he teach knowledge? And whom shall he make to*

understand doctrine? Them that are weaned from the milk, and drawn from the breasts.

10. *For precept must be upon precept, precept upon precept; line upon line, line upon line, here a little, and there a little.*

The Lord emphasizes over and over again to compare precepts in order to gain a thought or an idea from the Holy Spirit. Then He speaks of the future when His people will speak with stammering lips and another tongue. He is speaking to this generation; but to understand, you must hear every word and study it line upon line and precept upon precept.

Isaiah 28:11-13

11. *For with stammering lips and another tongue will he speak to his people.*

12. *To whom he said, This is the rest wherewith ye may cause the weary to rest; and this is the refreshing; yet they would not hear.*

13. *But the word of the Lord was upon them precept upon precept, precept upon precept line upon line, line upon line, here a little and there a little, that they might go, and fall backward, and be broken and scared and taken.*

These verses describe what began as habit for me. My way of worship and study of the Word of God. Some thought I was becoming a religious fanatic and needed psychological help. But this was the process of my hearing God and being obedient to all that was spoken to me.

As I look back, there seems to be many cases where the Bible became a Living Word as I was shown where to turn in scripture for answers. At other times, it has been like having a conversation with the Lord as I was led by His Word.

The Lord explained to me that He was fulfilling in this generation the greatest prophecy written in the scriptures, and no one understood it. The following are some of the highlights of what the Lord has spoken to me:

1. The Lord said, "Call My people the International Branch of the Lion of Judah."
2. The Lord said, "I am going to use you to help people all over the world in a financial way."
3. The Lord said, "I want you to write a book called *Thy Kingdom Come.*"
4. The Lord said, "Write and show My people how to become an army of God."
5. The Lord said, "You will be speaking from Jerusalem."
6. The Lord said, "Draw seven key people together. The Lord will speak to each of them."
7. The Lord said, "I place Myself at your command to fulfill all that I have spoken."
8. The Lord said, "Many will be brought in and many will be taken out."
9. The Lord said, "You are not to choose anyone. You have no control. This is being done by the Lord thy God."
10. The Lord said, "You are not to reach back and try to hold anyone up. I will take out and replace with another."

11. The Lord said, "I want My people to give Me their wills."
12. The Lord said, "I need people who will be obedient and move when I say move and stop when I say stop."

These are a few of the lines and precepts that I received over several years. Also included was personal information such as the names of people, then unknown to me, whom I would be working with later in my life.

* * *

My twin brother had a successful logging operation in Sitka, Alaska, and offered me a job. He offered to pay for my flight too. With all the prophetic messages I had received, I couldn't accept it. Members of my family thought that I had really gone off the deep end. But after making a commitment to follow the Lord, I had no choice but to be obedient to what I thought was the Lord's will.

It would be God's responsibility to provide the way and keep me alive according to the words spoken to me prophetically. And I trusted the Lord.

As Esther, the prophetess, continued to prophesy and pray for me, more information was being released line upon line and precept upon precept. It came bit by bit, a little bit here and a little bit there, as we met regularly for prayer.

Esther told me that the Lord had instructed her to tell me that I was to begin working on a plan He had developed for helping the people of the world. She said I was to begin with an astronomical amount of money–$4 billion.

I felt that the Lord wanted me to write the plan down so it would be clear in my mind.

Those whom the Lord brought forth into His plan would do the administration, management, and development. I could see that this was a worldwide plan to mobilize people of God around the world.

The realistic side of me also knew there would need to be a development plan and a feasibility study. I felt the Lord would want to help the poor and the needy of the world, and this became the basis of my understanding as I put together the plan.

People would be raised up with better food, clothing, housing, and employment. The many people participating in the plan of restoration would proclaim the gospel around the world.

As I was putting all of this into my mind, the Lord spoke through Esther and said, "Now I want you to multiply the amount of money by 100 times. Expand the project to $400 billion."

I was reminded of a scripture. It seemed that He was saying, "If I told you everything at once, you would not believe."

Habakkuk 1:5

5. *Behold ye among the heathen, and regard, and wonder marvelously: for I will work a work in your days, which you will not believe, though it be told you.*

The idea, the way I understood it, was to break huge parcels of undeveloped land into small parcels of five to ten acres. Each parcel would support one family unit sufficiently.

Each of the huge parcels would be set up as small self-supporting communities. None of the work was to be done by large multi-national companies or even very large equipment.

Hart, a friend of mine, helped develop a plan where each family would be given equipment, a few goats, a couple of cows, some chickens, a nice home, and the latest in agricultural training. Each property would have a central management team to coordinate the total community into a self-sustaining unit. I was taking this very seriously.

Once this plan was in place, the Lord spoke through Esther again and said that I would be meeting someone by the name of Doug who would be helping me. He said, "When you meet him, you must be very firm in telling him what I have said to you, and you must not take no for an answer."

I didn't know who or where Doug was.

The Lord always speaks a little bit at a time. He never gives you the whole picture all at once. Only a little bit here and a little bit there. Through all of this, I was being given a master's degree in patience. I continued to be motivated because I felt that the Lord was truly using me as a vehicle to help His people. He wanted me to find a way to help those that are less fortunate.

Being without money was not the hardest part. Waiting

for things to happen spiritually and seeing only the day-to-day trials of survival were the hardest parts for me.

No matter how I see the need or even a pending personal catastrophe, the Lord never seems to be in a hurry. My experience has been that the Lord is not inclined to speed up the pace, no matter how I feel or might plead. The timing is the Lord's, not ours.

Later, the Lord spoke to me through Esther saying that Beatrice was withholding information from me that I needed to know. Information that was to help me fulfill the Lord's plans.

I met with Beatrice in a Boise coffee shop along Broadway Avenue. I was frank with her and told her that I believed she was withholding information from me that was vital to the Lord's plan.

She said she couldn't remember anything that she thought I needed to know. I hadn't seen her for several weeks so we talked about other things. After about twenty minutes, she said, "Gary, I remember what it was."

She explained that she had taken a trip to Los Angeles to attend several church-related meetings. At one of these meetings was a young man whom she had a strange feeling about; and after the meeting, he turned to speak to her. I watched as she struggled to recount the conversation. Finally, she said, "His comment was: 'We have 14 billion dollars for His Kingdom. Do you know what I mean?'" She responded by saying it was for the Kingdom of God.

When I heard this, I was stunned. This was the information that I needed to begin the plan the Lord had directed me to fulfill. I quickly obtained the number of the young man from Beatrice and walked directly to the restaurant telephone.

A woman answered the phone and informed me that the person I wanted to speak to was in Europe. Then she asked, "Did you want to see him about international financing?" When I replied yes, she said there was someone else who might be able to help me. His name was Hal.

When I finally got in touch with Hal, I started out by giving him a testimony of everything that had led me to him. I explained how the Lord was leading each step I took. I also told him I had no money or assets.

Hal explained how this off-shore financing worked and how the large banks were paying higher rates of interest than the Arab nations were willing to lend money for.

The world's best prime rate of interest at that time was above 15%. This put the Moslem people in an awkward position. The Koran—the Islamic Bible—states that the followers of Islam should not charge interest. However, because of the high rate of inflation, if they did not charge interest, their fortunes would slowly fade away. As a result, the Arab nations were lending money at a rate several percentage points lower than what the world's largest banks were willing to pay in interest.

I then asked Hal if there was any way that I, an individual with no money, credit, or assets, could get such a loan. He replied that an individual's financial position didn't make any difference. The loans were made only when the loan was guaranteed by one of the hundred top-rated banks in the world. He said I needed to get a prime bank guarantee. I asked how I could get a prime bank guarantee without any assets.

He said I needed to talk to Doug at Financial Services in Newport Beach, California. *Doug?*

Hal then said, "After you get the prime bank guarantee from Doug, come back to me and I'll put you in contact with one of the men who handles the finances for these Middle Eastern nations."

Hal further explained that when a world prime bank agrees to accept a large amount of money into a savings account and guarantees to pay a set interest rate of 15%, the bank would be paying $15 million each year in interest on a $100 million deposit. Since the Arab banks only charge 7% interest, they only charge $7 million per year in interest.

Therefore, with the guaranteed $15 million per year income for 20 years, one can pay the interest on $200 million and have the reserve million applied toward the principal. The entire $200 million borrowed at 7% will be paid back by the interest received from the world prime bank. So $100 million can be used without worrying about debt service.

Of course, I was anxious to get to Newport Beach in California to see Doug. The very person that the Lord spoke of through Esther's prophecy. I decided to move to Los Angeles for a few months.

I had a couple friends who had moved to Los Angeles

shortly before I did. One of these friends, Larry, had arranged for housing in Los Angeles motels through a barter system of credit he had.

A few weeks after Larry left, I managed to put together $150 and headed to Los Angeles in my little Toyota. Once there, I got together with Larry and John, another friend, and they agreed to furnish me with a place to stay if I let them use my car as transportation when they needed it.

This worked well for a while. We managed to survive and lived together for about nine months. At the end of that time, we each went in different directions and I lost contact with them.

After I arrived in Los Angeles, I made arrangements to meet Doug at Financial Services. I went to see him as soon as I was settled.

I told him my story of how the Lord had given me his name and told me that he would help me. I told him the Lord had instructed me not to accept *no* as an answer.

He was confused and a little shaken, saying that he didn't know what to think about what I had just told him. I could certainly understand his uncertainty. I, myself, was more than a little confused at times. I think it is probably my determination and faith in the Lord that has helped me all these years in securing the aid that I needed from the various people I've come in contact with. In any case, he said I looked like a decent person and would see what he could do to help me.

He explained that he would get me a commitment from the tenth largest bank in the world at that time, the Hong

Kong Shan Hai Bank. He said that he would try to get a commitment for $500 million; and after we closed one account, we would keep going back and doing the same thing over again.

He explained his commission arrangements and said I needed to come up with $10,000 up front. And he wanted me to know that, after I got the guarantee, it was my responsibility to find the money source and have funds already committed to close before he would be able to place the guarantees.

Now I had to figure out how to get the investment money, which is always a risky situation for an investor.

*   *   *

Earl, a friend from Boise, helped me by putting up the capital I needed. I was able to secure a lawyer through a friend in New York, and he helped me to form a corporation as a legal entity. I was confident that the Lord would work through me in helping to get His project underway.

Peter, the attorney, said I needed to come up with a name for the corporation. The only name that was accepted was *Lion Branch International*. (In a prophetic message I later received, I was instructed to rename the project *The International Branch of the Lion of Judah*.)

I, of course, had my doubts about the feasibility of this plan. And I worried about where I was going to come up with the initial investment. But as I worked to fulfill the Lord's plan, it seemed that everything would just fall into place. If I was completely broke and felt that the Lord wanted me to do something, then I was somehow able to obtain the money I needed to complete what I was supposed to do.

At one point, while visiting my parents in Clarkston, Washington, sometime after I secured Peter's legal services, I visited with Mary, a long-time friend who was a real estate agent.

While there, Mary asked, "Gary, are you by any chance going to New York in the next couple of days? There's a ticket available from Spokane to New York for $25, but it's only good until Sunday night." I said I was planning to go to Luxembourg some time soon but wasn't sure exactly when. There was a person there whom I needed to speak to about this financial venture. I only had $27 at the time Mary mentioned this, so I didn't purchase the ticket.

About 8 p.m. on Sunday, I received a phone call from Esther. This was the only time she ever called me. She said the Lord wanted to speak to me and she started praying over the phone.

I was told that this was the time for me to go to New York and then on to Luxembourg. Someone in Luxembourg would be able to help me obtain the financing I needed to begin undertaking the Lord's plan. But there was a warning for me to be aware of a change in attitude.

This time, while Esther was praying, she began having a vision, which she proceeded to describe to me. She saw the people in New York huddled in a meeting. One of them was trying to persuade the others that I had taken too much upon myself over the potential finances that were being sought for the Kingdom of God. This person was saying that wisdom comes from the council of many.

I was cautioned by the Lord that I had received instructions from Him, and I had to be firm and could not turn to the right nor to the left.

After this telephone call, I packed my bags to go. It was 9 p.m. Sunday·evening and I had $27. Sunday was the last day that the ticket was available and Clarkston is over 100 miles from the Spokane International Airport. It would be impossible to do anything this late.

I know that when the Lord is doing something, opposition will come. But if I am obedient and walk in faith and don't quit or change my mind, miracles can happen. If it is of God, nothing can stop it; and if it is not of God, nothing can make it happen.

I called the number Mary had given me of the ticket holder and told him that I would buy the ticket if he were able to get the ticket changed to the 7 a.m. Monday morning flight. He said he would try.

He called me back in a few minutes, saying he had been successful. I then called Mike, the friend who had helped me secure Peter's legal services, in New York and asked if I could stay with him, which he agreed to.

Before I left, my brother gave me $60. So after I bought the ticket to New York, I had $62 in my pocket when I boarded the plane. I was on my way to New York and from there to Luxembourg.

*   *   *

Upon arriving at Mike's door in Manhattan, it became apparent that there had been a drastic change in Mike's involvement in this plan.

Mike questioned me about the position the Lord had placed me in, and he said that he and Peter should share the position and responsibility with me. He said all decisions should be decided by a majority vote of the three. He explained this was the way it should be according to the Bible scriptures and principles of the way God does things.

He then informed me that he had arranged a meeting with the assistant pastor of the Manhattan Baptist Church for a counseling session.

I was reminded of the man of God that was sent to deliver a message to King Jeroboam. Specific instructions were given that he should not eat nor drink, and he was not to return the same route that he had taken in coming.

An old prophet had heard of this man of God and went to him. He invited the young man to come and eat with him. At first the man of God refused, saying that the Lord had forbidden him to eat in the town.

Then the old prophet said, "I am a prophet also." This statement caused the man of God to be intimidated and he accepted the old prophet's invitation.

The disobedience of this man of God resulted in his death. While eating with the old prophet, the Lord spoke through the old prophet to the man of God and said, "Because you have been disobedient to the word of the Lord, when you leave here, you will be killed by a lion."

When the man of God left, he was slain by a lion just as the old prophet had said.

I was determined to be obedient to what I had been told, regardless of any pressure from outside sources.

After the meeting at the Baptist church, there was a lot of tension between Mike and me. The next morning, when we met with Peter, I carried my luggage with me.

Peter's convictions were as strong as mine were; we agreed to disagree. I left all the corporate papers on his desk unsigned. It seemed the Lord now had other plans. At times, I'm not sure exactly what it is that the Lord wants of me. I was confused but knew that my job was simply to follow, unconditionally, the plan the Lord sets before me.

I spent two nights at the YMCA for $16 per night before I ran out of money. I then moved out to the La Guardia Airport while I still had bus fare. I placed a few calls and made my bed on a couple chairs. I wanted people, such as Beatrice, to know where I was in case any funds became available.

Within a few days, money started arriving. I felt that God was working through my family and friends to help me accomplish His mission. The airport's Western Union had $50 for me. Then $100. After a few days I had nearly $400. I checked every airline to see what might be the least expensive fair to Luxembourg. Icelandic Air had a one-way ticket for $189, and I was off to Luxembourg.

In Luxembourg, I stayed one night in a hotel and had two meetings with a gentleman by the name of Brian. Brian told me that I was asking for the impossible. He said that since the trust officers of the Middle Eastern banks have the money, they require that the guarantees be placed in a trust bank before they will confirm funding and that there were no exceptions.

This was exactly the same conversation that I had had with Doug. Neither party would be the first to commit. I had to obtain one thing before the other, and it seemed impossible to obtain either one.

Knowing that nothing could be done, I was wondering why the Lord had sent me to Luxembourg. But I had learned that the greater the problem or opposition, the greater the miracles. I came to the conclusion that opposition is a very positive sign; and if I were obedient to the Lord, I could always be sure that the Lord would perform miracles to accomplish His purpose.

I decided to go back home. There was nothing else I could do in Luxembourg. When I got to the airport, there was a flight boarding for Chicago. It appeared that it was perfect timing. I rushed to the ticket counter and emptied all my foreign money on the counter.

The lady counted the money and said I was short of having enough money by quite a lot. I asked about a flight to New York. I prayed I had enough.

The ticket was $256, but the plane didn't leave until the following morning. I was worried that I wouldn't have enough money to get me back to the United States. I emptied my pockets of every bill and coin I could find. Again, the Lord was with me. I had enough for the ticket and $5 left over.

The woman behind the counter looked worriedly at me and asked what I would do until the next morning's flight.

"You don't even have cab fare, and they will not let you stay in the airport here like they do in New York. They kick everyone out at 11 p.m.," she said.

I looked skeptically outside and saw the cold November rain coming down. I remembered what the Lord had said through Esther as she prayed that Sunday night before I left Spokane. "You will know that I am with you on this trip because when you see the rain, you know that My spirit is upon you." I then realized that it had rained when I left Spokane. It had rained every day nonstop while I was in New York. And in Luxembourg, there had been steady rain. I couldn't remember one moment it had not been raining.

Eleven o'clock rolled around, and I watched nervously as they began demanding that everyone leave the airport. Anyone who hesitated was ushered to the door physically. Several young people with backpacking gear were pushed out into the rain. A kind-looking airport security guard approached me, said I had to leave the terminal, and ushered me to the door gently. As we neared the door, he turned to me and said, in a conspiring tone, to go to the dining room upstairs and bring down two chairs. I was tired and cold and didn't look forward to the prospect of sleeping out in the cold November rain, so I was quick to follow his cryptic instructions. I trusted the Lord.

When I obediently returned with the two chairs, he had me put them between two sets of sliding glass doors. It was the breezeway that kept the wind from blowing into the terminal. Only one door was allowed to open at a time.

He said, "You can use these two chairs and sit all night between these two sets of sliding glass doors. You'll be locked out of the terminal, but you'll still be out of the cold and rain."

I praised the Lord. The Lord had performed another miracle to keep me warm and dry. I don't know why I, out of all the people in the airport that night, was chosen to be allowed to sleep inside the doors. Perhaps it was my faith in the Lord that helped me through all these trials. In any case, I felt the Lord's presence with me that night and was grateful for His blessing.

*   *   *

After returning from Luxembourg, I spent a month in Clarkston, Washington. Then a couple of weeks in Boise, Idaho, before going back to Los Angeles.

When I finally returned to Los Angeles, I was out of money and had no place to stay. John and Larry had moved on. I was totally alone and waiting upon the Lord for a miracle. It seemed like everything I was doing was falling apart.

I continued working to secure a prime bank guarantee. Each time I contacted Doug, it seemed he was getting less cooperative with my efforts. I know he probably thought I was nuts, and I prayed to the Lord to give me strength.

Several months had passed since going to see Brian in Luxembourg, and there seemed no way of getting anything done. Then the Lord spoke an important message, but at the time unbelievable to me.

I was told that the Lord had changed Brian's heart and I was to call him. He would give me all the information I needed to know.

As I wondered what I could say to Brian, I remembered an incident at my first meeting with him in Luxembourg. I had just met Brian in his office and had given him a testimony of all the Lord had done.

Brian listened patiently to my story, then excused himself, stepped out of the room, and talked privately to his associate. The door wasn't completely shut, and I could hear bits of the conversation. I smiled as I heard Brian say, "But the guy isn't crazy, he's a nice guy."

This encouraged me. In that one sentence, he was defending me to his associate and not passing judgment. He must have considered that this may be a work of God. It was recollecting these thoughts that gave me the courage to place the call to Brian.

When I reached him, I asked him if he might have thought of any way he could confirm the funding of $500 million so that Doug could put the prime bank guarantee in place.

Brian answered, "You know I can't give you the names of bankers to verify funding prior to having the collateral put in place."

I didn't know what to say. There were several moments

of intense, awkward silence on the line between us. Brian finally broke the awkward moment by saying gently, "I know you're a man of God. I'll give you the information you need, Gary. Keep in mind, though, that the people you are dealing with that have the collateral (those at Financial Services in L.A.) will try to cut you out and go around you. They want the loan for themselves."

I couldn't see Doug doing that, and besides, his commission would have been fairly large.

After these warnings, Brian gave me the bank name, address, officers' names, and the account numbers where these funds could be verified. When I took this information to Doug, he told me that the bank didn't exist. Now what?

I headed for the Los Angeles Library and asked for the banker's almanac. There I found all the registered banks in the world listed. Among them was the bank that Brian had given me the information about. I copied everything about the bank–its size, status, bank officers' names, etc.

I took this information back to Doug. He seemed surprised and excited at the same time. It was up to Doug now, and I decided not to bother him for a week while he made the arrangements to close the loan.

I spent the week planning each step of where the funds should be deposited for the greatest safety. I planned how I would ask certain individuals to a private retreat for a time of prayer and planning to see what the Lord would want us to do step by step.

After a week went by, I called Doug to see if he had confirmed the funds in this bank-to-bank communications, and I wanted to know if he had a closing date.

When I asked to speak to Doug, his personal secretary told me that he was meeting with some banking officials in Mexico. When I heard this, I knew something was wrong. We'd been working on this project for more than a year, and he was going to make about $20 million in commission. He would not be in Mexico if this were about ready to close.

I was in a state of frustration and needed guidance from the Lord. I called Esther at her home in Boise. I was told that Doug was in Luxembourg, trying to cut us out of the loan and collect the fallout from the arbitrage for himself. It appears that the Lord had given me information through Brian that even the bankers in the United States didn't know about getting funding from Middle Eastern nations.

Then the Lord said, through Esther, that Doug's secretary, Gerry, was very upset over what he was doing and that she was considering quitting her job because of his asking her to lie to me. I felt that the Lord wanted me to talk with her and tell her how much He loved her.

A few days later, I met with Gerry and told her all that the Lord had told me. I was careful not to place her in a compromising position of being disloyal to her employer.

I told her she did not need to say anything, but that I was aware of her feelings when Doug had asked her to lie and that I knew she was considering quitting her job.

When I told her that the Lord had sent me to tell her that He loved her, she said with tears in her eyes, "Who am I that God would do this for me?"

As I was leaving, I said, "Gerry, I have told you all the Lord has told me to tell you. You can prove that this is all wrong by saying that Doug is in Mexico as I told you."

Gerry looked at me with tears in her eyes and said, "Everything you've said sounds pretty right to me."

* * *

Over the years, I've learned that waiting gives me great revelation and understanding of the mysteries in the Lord's Word, the Bible. It seems great understanding is revealed during times of great pressure.

After this meeting with Gerry, I did not call or speak to Doug for a while. I knew it was not God's will for me to confront him or accuse him. But one day, I called Esther and asked her to pray. The Lord spoke and I was told that Doug had been given a piece of paper that the Lord had instructed him to give to me. I had no idea what it might be. I wondered briefly if it might be something he had received in Luxembourg.

I was told to go to his office and ask for the piece of paper. When I did, Doug denied having any paper that was meant for me. I left the office frustrated and confused.

I again called Esther and when she prayed, the Lord said, "Go back and ask him again for that paper. It is right on his desk."

So I went to see Doug a second time, this time with slightly less conviction. When I asked for the piece of paper again, he repeated that he didn't have any idea what I was talking about. His tone and manner were more agitated than before.

When I spoke to Esther a third time, she said the Lord had told her I was to go back yet again. "But this time," she said, "ask him to open the third drawer down on the left side of his desk and give you the top paper."

I was told that Doug knew what he was to give me and had hidden it. As I was hearing this, I was thinking to myself, *Lord, I might not be able to do this. Now the whole office probably thinks I'm a nut case.*

I swallowed my pride and approached Doug for the third time. I felt like a complete fool by now, but I was determined to be obedient to the Lord. I told Doug that the paper I needed was in the third drawer down on the left side of his desk.

He left the small conference room where we were talking and returned with a handwritten paper, which he grudgingly handed to me.

Doug then asked me if any of the three names meant anything to me. After looking at them, I said, "No, they don't mean anything to me, but I'm still supposed to have them."

I later came to recognize one of the names as the President of Saudi Arabia, another was the financial advisor, and the third was the financial administrator. I recognized the financial administrator's name from a story featured in *Time Magazine* that stated he was handling the nation's finances through selective middlemen. The handwritten paper also mentioned an office in Zug, Switzerland.

I know all of this may sound odd to you—the way things kept falling into place for me. I now had the names of the people who could potentially secure the money necessary to fulfill what I believed to be the Lord's desires. Keep in mind that it was strange for me too. At times, I wasn't sure what to think about this whole thing. I knew that the Lord had plans for me, and I just wanted to follow His instructions and see where they led me.

I called Esther and asked her to pray. I had no idea what to do with this new information. The Lord said through Esther, "I will send you to see this man, and you will receive a large amount of money from him for My Kingdom. This man is a Muslim, but he knows Me in his own way. You are to tell him all that I have done through you. But you are not to go until I tell you to go. Just carry this paper in your wallet until I tell you to go see him."

*   *   *

During these periods of waiting, I spent my time seeking the Lord and trying to find hidden meanings in the scriptures.

My friend Patty moved from Boise, Idaho, to Arcadia, California, and she introduced me to a family who later invited me to come and stay in an extra bedroom they had in their home. They unselfishly opened their home to me and became very special friends whom I greatly respected.

I tried, over a period of several years, to obtain funding through other various sources. At one point, the Lord led me to a television ministry consisting of two churches called *Lift Jesus Higher.* I thought that perhaps this was God's purpose for me—at least at this point in my life. I wanted to help people and knew that I could with the Lord's strength and guidance.

I had arranged meetings with a group of insurance companies in Los Angeles who were considering working with us. In the end, it was not the Lord's will to allow the insurance companies to help *Lift Jesus Higher.*

Afterwards, I was really searching for guidance from the Lord. A friend, who knew of my distress, came to me with a scripture.

Isaiah 41:10
10. *Fear thou not; for I am with thee: be not dismayed; for I am God; I will strengthen thee; yea, I will help thee; yea I will uphold thee with the right hand of my righteousness.*

After reading it, I experienced renewed energy. Sometimes a word of encouragement does wonders.

I eventually left *Lift Jesus Higher.* I felt that the Lord wanted me to move on. I moved to Phoenix, Arizona, and I was able to stay with my dear friends, John and Sharon. We all attended high school together in Lewiston, Idaho. John was the one who first led me to the Lord in 1968 by sharing the *Four Spiritual Laws* booklet with me.

About a month after arriving in Phoenix, I attended the Valley Cathedral Church. Another divine appointment took place as a woman named Marilyn sat down beside me in a crowd of about 4,000 people.

I found Marilyn to be a very special person with the gift of prophecy. As we shared with each other, she said, "This seems to be a fulfillment of what the Lord showed me twenty years ago."

The things the Lord had been telling her and doing through her matched perfectly with all that the Lord was speaking to me and doing in my life.

As I came to know and worship with my new friends in Phoenix, the Lord began speaking to Marilyn. She revealed to me a vision she had received many years earlier that was to be fulfilled by helping me.

The Lord spoke through Marilyn, saying that I would be going to Jerusalem, and the Lord had her prepare the way for me to go. She sacrificed all her money and credit sources to carry out the fulfillment of God's will for this trip.

Before leaving on this trip, I didn't have a full understanding of the purpose of it. Why was I going to Jerusalem? What did the Lord desire of me? However, before leaving on this trip, the Lord gave explicit directions of how I was to pray over the city of Jerusalem.

Even to this day, I don't have a full understanding of all that this trip meant, but I walked the streets of Jerusalem and prayed to myself while visiting all the places described in the Bible.

Zechariah 2:1-5
1. *I lifted up mine eyes again, and looked and behold a man with a measuring line in his hand.*

2. *Then said I, Whither goest thou? And he said unto me, To measure Jerusalem, to see what is the breadth thereof, and what is the length thereof.*

3. *And, behold, the angel that talked with me went forth, and another angel went out to meet him,*

4. *And said unto him, Run, speak to this young man, saying, Jerusalem shall be inhabited as towns without walls for the multitude of men and cattle therein:*

5. *For I, sayeth the Lord, will be unto her a wall of fire round about, and will be the glory in the midst of her.*

On the day I went to Jerusalem, Marilyn arranged for the round trip ticket. I didn't have any money at all. Marilyn knew I probably didn't have money for rent or food either. She was very kind and did everything she could to help me. She truly believed, as I did, that I was appointed by God to help the less fortunate people of the world.

As she drove me to the airport, Marilyn said, "The Lord just spoke to me. I don't know how much money I have in my purse, but I know I have some bills and loose change. The Lord said, 'Give Gary $99.'" She stopped the car and counted all her money out to me, including all of her change. It was exactly $99.

*   *   *

The flight to Jerusalem was rather uneventful. I arrived safely and began establishing myself for what I thought would be a short visit.

I met an old man while in Jerusalem who seemed kind,

but caused me a great deal of spiritual pain. He offered me a place to stay after I ran out of money, and I thought this was an answer to my prayers.

This man, however, turned out to be a thief. Not only did he steal from others, he stole from me. He stole my airline ticket home. I was stuck in Jerusalem with no money and no way to get back home. I prayed to the Lord for guidance and strength.

I went to the airlines daily, as well as the United State's Embassy, trying to explain what was happening. But no one would help me. I was able to work four hours a day cleaning up a youth hostel in exchange for a bed and one meal a day.

After six weeks, the airlines finally gave me a ticket back to Phoenix. When I got to the airport, I was informed there were two people by the name of Gary Larrabee trying to board the flight to Phoenix. Evidently, the old man was trying to leave the country by using my name and the stolen ticket.

The airport security checked me out with a fine tooth comb and eventually let me board the flight. I never saw the old man again. I often wonder what happened to him and what the Lord was trying to teach me by bringing him into my life. Perhaps there are some things we will never understand.

About a year after this trip, Marilyn and I were praying together. The Lord started speaking through her about the Branch and the Lord said, "The Branch was planted in Jerusalem by Gary's praying over Jerusalem. Neither of you had a full understanding, but both of you were obedient as I knew you would be."

After receiving this word from the Lord, the seventeenth chapter of Ezekiel seemed to be a parable of Israel's history. These verses seem both prophetic and historic:

> *But the eagle cropped of the twigs, the remnant of the lost tribes and planted in a fruitful field by great waters . . .*

(A land of traffic with a city of merchants could very well describe the ten tribes being in America and the eagle as the symbol of America.)

> *. . . and because of prosperity, these twigs [the people] lean to another eagle [or the world].*

This cedar is rebellious spiritually and becomes materialistic.

However, the last three verses may refer to the planting of the Branch in Jerusalem.

Ezekiel 17:22-24
22. *Thus sayeth the Lord God; I will also take of the highest branch of the high cedar and will set it; I will crop off from the top of his young twigs a tender one, and will plant it upon a high mountain and eminent.*
23. *In the mountain of height of Israel will I plant it: and it shall bring forth boughs, and her fruit, and be a goodly cedar; in the shadow of the branches there shall they dwell.*
24. *And all the trees of the field shall know that I the Lord have*

bought down the high tree, have exalted the low tree, have dried up the green tree, and have made the dry tree to flourish: I the Lord have spoken and have done it.

*   *   *

I got a job driving a city bus in Phoenix for a while. I found an apartment and made new friends at church. I attended men's meetings where I was able to give my testimony.

There were many people that God used to help me in gaining knowledge and understanding of His word. Many words of prophecy were spoken at churches and in smaller meetings that I believed were related to what I was doing. I learned a new precept of understanding.

The assistant pastor's wife at the church I attended had become acquainted with Marilyn. At one time I met with both Marilyn and the pastor's wife, and explained about the time several years ago when I was given the list of names from Doug at Financial Services.

One day the assistant pastor's wife called me to say that she and a small group of others had been praying about my situation. She believed that the Lord wanted to reveal to me a time when I was supposed to meet with the financial administrator in Zug, Switzerland. *So this was it, I thought.*

When I went to meet with them in their home and prayed for a word from the Lord, the Lord spoke to me personally and said, "You are supposed to go in a few months. Go on October 6, 1987." I had been carrying this information in my wallet for six years.

Until now, nothing had been truly successful in accomplishing the Lord's plan. I was determined to be prepared. I wanted to know how to communicate, so I read through the Koran and discovered that Muslims also believe in Moses and Jesus. They don't believe Jesus is the Son of God, yet they believe that Jesus was the Word and the Word created all things.

Six years earlier, the Lord spoke of one of the men listed on the paper and said, "This man knows Me in his own way, and you will share everything I have told you with him." I needed to know how to communicate.

With $10 in my wallet and only a week away from the date of departure, I decided to part with $7 to attend the Arizona Breakfast Club meeting. I needed inspiration and felt that this meeting would somehow help me. The Lord seemed to be drawing me to the meeting.

There were about 300 people at the meeting, and they asked everyone who had come for the first time to stand and introduce themselves.

A lady sitting a few seats away stood up. She said, "My name is Mary. I'm from Bracketsville, Texas, and I came all the way to Phoenix just to attend this breakfast club meeting."

During the meeting, the Lord impressed to me that I needed to talk to this lady. After the meeting, I introduced myself to her and said I believed the Lord was telling me I needed to speak to her. She answered by saying, "It's strange you should say that because I feel the same way. I believe I am supposed to talk to you too."

After we were seated at a private table, we began talking. She said that she went into her backyard garden daily to pray, and the Lord spoke to her there.

She said that she was told to go to Phoenix, Arizona, to attend the Arizona Breakfast Club meeting. She was told that she was to deliver a message to someone she would meet there. Then she said, "I believe you are that person."

She said, "You are going someplace for an important meeting. But things are not going to happen the way that you expect. You are to put everything down that you want to say in writing."

I told her of all the events in my life—how I had been led to Doug and how I got this man's name out of the third drawer on the left side of his desk.

To my surprise, she knew of the type of financing that I was trying to secure.

I couldn't believe my eyes when the meeting was over. She reached into her purse and handed me $800.

After this, there seemed to be a great difference in my credibility among my friends. I heard the same thing over and over, "Gary, we've heard all your stories, but we see you are always broke, always in some struggle. But now, we see evidence that this may very well be a work of the Lord."

My friends started handing me money for the trip to Switzerland. On October 6, 1987, I had $4,000 to purchase my ticket and board the plane.

* * *

My flight took me to Zurich, Switzerland. The train system in Zurich ran beneath the airport, so I just carried my bags several stories underground and boarded the train to Zug to look for a company called Pimex Finanz.

Zug is a small lake town, and its primary business seems to be banking. Several blocks consist of nothing but banking establishments. I checked into a hotel and hit the streets, hoping to find English-speaking people to tell me where Pimex Finanz was.

I spent the day making the rounds to all the banks. No one would tell me anything. I covered the town, then decided to make the same rounds again the next day.

The second day, a lady at one of the banks said to me, "You know, of course, that even if I do know who you are looking for, I can't tell you?" I was aware of secret bank accounts but not secret *banks*. In any case, I got the picture.

Now what should I do? I was certainly not going back to Phoenix empty-handed. I was pressed to fly to London. There was one person I knew there, someone I met when I was in Jerusalem. Her name was Susan.

Susan and I had spent some time together in Jerusalem and had become quite good friends. She wrote to me after I returned to Arizona, and told me how she was attending church and how her life had changed as a result of her trip to Jerusalem. She gave me her address in London at that time; and after I arrived, I tried to get in touch with her. On the second day, I was able to make contact with her, and she introduced me to some of her friends.

The husband of one of her friends was well-versed in international finances, and he ended up being a great help to me. They had an extra bedroom in their house and invited me to stay with them while I was in London. I'm not sure why I felt I needed to be in London. I only knew that the Lord wanted me there. He would reveal His reasons in His own time. Susan's friends were struggling financially, so I bought much of the food while I was there.

Susan showed me how to get around London, and she helped me as we went to every Arab bank, embassy, and government agency we could find.

Finally, at an Arab tourist agency, I asked a lady about the man listed on the paper and she said, "Oh, you want to see the Governor." After a thorough investigation, I was able to obtain a phone number for him in Saudi Arabia.

When I finally reached him, I told him that Allah (Allah is the name used by Muslims to refer to God) had given me his name, that this was a divine appointment, and I wanted to meet with him. He listened patiently and then requested that I send everything to him in writing first.

I had already prepared everything I needed in writing due to Mary's advice prior to my leaving. I was encouraged. While I waited for him to respond to what I sent, I kept in touch with the wonderful assistant pastor and his wife in Phoenix, Arizona. We all felt that I would probably need to go to Saudi Arabia, and they sent me an additional $1,200 to make the trip.

The day the money arrived, the man of the house where

I was staying informed me that he and his wife were going to have all of their household furnishings repossessed the next day, unless they could get 800 English pounds, the exact equivalent of $1,200. He knew I had the money, and I'm sure he hoped I would be able to help them. I was torn. These people had been so kind to me. They'd taken me in when I had nowhere to go. But I also felt that the Lord wanted me to complete this mission.

I explained what he already knew, that I was on a mission and that the money was sent to me to finish my mission. The only thing I knew to do was pray and do whatever I thought the Lord wanted me to.

The next morning I rose early and walked down to a McDonald's restaurant a few blocks away to have coffee. When I returned, I found out that he had called Saudi Arabia and found out that the man I wanted to see was with a delegation of people at the Regenes Hotel in London.

Five minutes later, the van showed up in front of the home to repossess the furniture. I reached into my wallet and handed him $1,200—absolutely sure I was doing the right thing. I dressed in my best suit and headed for the Regenes Hotel, hoping for the best.

When I got to the Regenes, the front desk told me that there was an entourage of Saudi Sheiks staying there but they were not in at the time. I waited in the hotel lobby until 9 p.m., to no avail, then decided to go back to the house and try to call him.

It was after 10 p.m. when I made the call. He answered

the phone by saying that he was in bed. My response was that Allah had sent me on a mission and I was supposed to talk to him. Once he realized who I was, we had a very professional conversation.

He said he had received and read all that I had sent to him. He then said, "What makes you think I can come up with $400 billion?" I told him that Allah told me he could.

My parting words to him were that if he had read what I sent him, I had completed my mission and would leave the results to Allah. It was time to go home.

When I got back to Phoenix and recounted my experiences to my friends, they were disappointed. I was somewhat disappointed too. Nothing much had come of the trip, though I felt that I had done what the Lord desired of me. My friends seemed to feel that I had made a poor judgment in giving away the $1,200 that had been sent to me in order to complete a mission.

Truthfully, in spite of the comments I received, I would probably do the same thing again. I believed I *had* completed the mission. It was up to the Lord now. And it felt good being able to help my friends. I can rest easy knowing that they at least still have a roof over their heads.

*   *   *

The pursuit of seeking finances for the Kingdom of God is still an ongoing mission for me. I'm still waiting upon the Lord for the next move. Anyone being led by the Spirit of the Lord learns that, no matter how much of a hurry we are in, the Lord seems to have plenty of time. There is no way to hurry Him up.

When there is no movement, all you can do is stop and wait for the Lord. My life may seem like it's out of control, but it is a life under perfect control—not my control, but in submission and fully committed to the Kingdom of God. My responsibility is to be obedient to the Spirit of the Lord and leave the results to God.

PART II

Now that I have told the story of how my mission began, I want to explain how I came upon a new understanding of some prophetic scriptures that will be explained in the next several chapters. We all seem to be guilty of thinking someone else has a better understanding of scriptures. We look at a difficult scripture and listen as others explain it to us. I was uncomfortable with some explanations that were traditionally understood.

Some explanations simply didn't line up, in my mind at least, with scripture, regardless of how well they were explained. As the Lord began leading me on this mission, He said, "I am bringing forth My people from around the world to fulfill the greatest prophecy in the Bible, but no one understands it." At this point, I set aside everything I had been traditionally taught and said, "Teach me, Lord."

The Lord continues to teach me, and there is still a great deal that I don't fully understand. So I will state my present understanding, reserving the right to adjust my understanding to further truths of scripture yet to be revealed.

Getting started right is very important in any journey.

THE RIGHT START

Because of many generations of misunderstanding the Branch, described in Isaiah 11:1, we need to be sure exactly what each word of this verse means. In the past, because of the power, authority, wisdom, righteousness, etc. described in the first five verses it was nearly impossible to think that this could refer to anyone other than Jesus Christ. Subsequently, teachers put a false spin on this verse similar to the spin we see on the events of the daily news by commentators in the media.

> *Isaiah 11: 11*
> 11. *And there shall come forth a ROD out of the STEM OF JESSE and a BRANCH shall grow out of HIS ROOTS.*

Going backwards, we see the ROOTS belong to HIS, and HIS refers to the ROOTS. The ROOTS belong to the BRANCH, and the BRANCH refers to the ROD that came out of the STEM OF JESSE.

David is the Stem of Jesse. The Rod here refers to Jesus Christ. The Branch is all the followers of Jesus Christ.

So we must be clear that the Branch represents the followers of Jesus Christ, regardless of how powerful and glorious the description. But the power and authority are not from the Branch. The authority is Jesus Christ, the Rod, who holds all power and authority to give this power and authority to anyone He desires to give it to. He chooses to give all this power and authority to His people or His church, so that He may rule through His body, the Branch. He is the Vine, and we are the Branches.

When we totally submit to the power and the authority of Jesus Christ, we are saying a divine "yes" to be used by Him. By giving total submission, we will receive total power and authority in the name of Jesus. Through God's divine plan of submission and prayer, He is actually inviting us, as redeemed men and women of God, into a joint venture with Him. We are being asked to become a part of fulfilling a plan of God that was made, even before creation.

All the responsibility of implementing and fulfilling God's decisions is the responsibility of His servants here on Earth. The power, responsibility, and authority for enforcement will rest upon the followers of Christ, His anointed BRANCH, both corporately and individually.

We can't do this by our own power or might, but only through the Spirit of the Lord working in and through us. You might say that the key to opening the doors into the Millennial Kingdom is understanding how to let Jesus Christ open the door of the Kingdom through us, by our total submission.

Jesus is giving us this full power and authority, although we have not yet been able to accept it. He said, "As the Father has sent Me, even so, I send you." We, as His Branch, will be commissioned to reclaim, to judge, and govern the Kingdom with the full integrity of God Himself acting through us in the power of the seven spirits of the

Lord, described in Isaiah 11:1-5.

If we of this generation refuse to pray and submit to where we can be used, God will not bring this forth in this generation. He will never go beyond the will of His people on Earth to act. This does not mean the plan changes. His plan was made before the creation of the world, and His plan will never change. If we fail to act, the plan will merely be held up for a new generation. We don't want to make the mistake of the generation coming out of Egypt and roam in the wilderness of confusion for another forty years.

When God cannot find anyone on Earth suitable through total submission and willingness to act on His behalf, His program is suspended for a time. He waits until mankind gets back in proper alignment with Him in order to be used by Him to accomplish His perfect will. The blueprints of God's plan on Earth were drawn by Him at the beginning of time, and His plan will never change.

At the point He finds a person so willing that he has truly died to the *self*, when it is no longer he, but Christ, who lives in him to do His purposes, all the power of the universe will be available to him. The power will be in his spoken word, in the name of Jesus, to do great exploits in the will and name of Jesus Christ.

The world has not yet seen what the Lord will do through his totally submissive body.

International Branch of the Lion of Judah

God conceived the plan that this generation is to fulfill, even before He created the Earth. The plan for this generation to bring forth the Kingdom of God is recorded in the scriptures. The Lord has opened up the Word of God to me through much fasting and prayer. He has spoken to me through His prophetic word to help prepare this generation to reclaim all that has been stolen from us by the forces of evil.

Over the past twenty years, I have studied line upon line and precept upon precept. The prophetic word and revelation come only in parts, and all things must line up perfectly with the Word of God. If I have written anything that is not in perfect alignment with the Word of God, it is incorrect. Please bring any point of error to me, and state my error by scripture, not tradition.

There seem to be two reasons for the work the Lord is doing:

1. To have all power, all authority, all glory, and all honor be given to the Son, Jesus Christ.
2. To make the body of Christ His body and to make man like Christ.

In an earlier age, Satan, who had been given the high honor of an archangel, rebelled. He became jealous and wished to exalt himself to be equal with the Son of God. One-third of the angelic hosts followed in rebellion against

God. Satan's rebellion hurled everything into chaos.

God, therefore, created man with the same life and glory of Christ so that man might reclaim and bring all things back to God.

In Adam's original state, he was united with God and could have been used to deal with Satan's rebellion. But upon the failure of Adam's sin, he became separated and this created an additional problem. Mankind needed to be redeemed to where he could again deal with Satan's rebellion and reclaim all things back to God.

In order to realize God's purposes and deal with the problems, the Lord Jesus came down from Heaven to become man and accomplish the work of redemption. Christ resolved every problem on the cross. He crushed the head of the serpent, thus dealing with Satan's rebellion. He also redeemed the fallen race and reconciled all things to Himself. Through the cross, He imparts His life to men that they might again be like Him.

The Kingdom of God for this generation is to manifest the redemption and victory, which Christ has achieved, and reveal the execution of God's authority and power through His BRANCH, His body. We, of this generation, are to fulfill His eternal plan and purpose.

God is now bringing forth His overcomers—the faithful few to represent the church in the victory of Christ. These overcomers are not some special class, but simply a group of people who desire to be in God's perfect will and to be used by Him. These overcomers will not regard themselves as overcomers, but will recognize themselves as being nothing. They will have the reality, yet not the name, of overcomers.

God's overcomers will know and use the power and the authority of Christ Jesus. They will defeat Satan by using the authority in commanding and believing prayers.

God is now calling forth His overcomers to defeat Satan and reclaim all things to Christ Jesus.

Are you willing to become an overcomer?

Your armament is the blood of the Lamb of God, and you must maintain an attitude of having no fear of death.

STATEMENT OF MY PRESENT UNDERSTANDING

I have had a hunger for the Word of God since 1968, and the Lord has blessed me by revealing much to me in understanding prophetic scripture. Please test every word with scripture. I will try to explain what God has revealed to me concerning what lies ahead for this generation. I hope that this will be an encouragement to the body of Christ. Please hear me through before passing judgment. I don't claim to be a prophet: however, I do try to be sensitive to whatever the Lord may speak to me through His Spirit. The key to my understanding has been much fasting, praying in the Spirit, and waiting patiently for the Lord's timing.

When the Lord speaks, no matter how it sounds, I write it down and wait—leaving everything to the Lord. Sometimes in my own mind, it doesn't make sense for years; and then all at once, the Lord gives further revelation at His time.

- On April 10, 1984, I was told that the tribulation described in the Book of Revelation was beginning.
- On April 10, 1987, I was told that the vials were being poured forth.
- On June 13, 1984, I was told that the four angels were being placed at the four corners of the Earth. This seems to be the beginning point of the sealing of those referred to as the 144,000.

I know that you are wondering how this could be. The tribulation is only seven years and it has been more than twice that length of time and we are still here.

The First Seal

On April 10, 1984, the first seal was released. Think of this as a very slow leak in your car tire. The air comes out ever so slowly, and you are able to drive quite normally for a long period. But the air is slowly coming out just the same; and when it eventually becomes totally flat, you will no longer be able to drive.

The man on the white horse, described in Revelation 6:1-2, is a picture of a powerful body of believers in Jesus Christ. This is not the anti-christ. This is that perfect body of Christ, all in one mind and accord, all in total submission to the head.

The body of Christ is coming into unity by judgment. Judgment begins at the house of God and since April 10, 1984, all believers, organizations, or denominations have been under severe judgment in breaking the body. All true believers are being broken to the point of dying to *self*—to the point it is no longer I, but Christ, that lives in me. I can no longer live this life by myself.

Through much prayer for understanding, I started putting precept upon precept and came up with conclusions that I put on the shelf of my understanding. I waited upon the Lord for further understanding and direction as to what to do with this information.

It was a correct conclusion. However, it didn't happen the way I expected.

The Second Seal

This was not a good thing that was released on October 10, 1984, when the Lamb of God opened this seal. This seal took peace from the Earth, and power was given to people to kill one another. This was about the time when the barracks and the American troops were bombed in Lebanon. This was the point when terrorist threats to the world began increasing at an alarming rate.

The Third Seal

Now to the third seal—a very positive seal to the body of Christ.

The man on the black horse has a pair of balances and says a measure of wheat for a penny, and three measures of barley for a penny, and hurt not the oil and the wine.

This is the fulfillment of the wealth of the unrighteous stored up for the righteous. These balances are just balances. In that day, a measure was 6.25 bushels of dry measure or 58 gallons of liquid measure. The oil and the wine represent the believers being led by the Spirit of the Lord and not the wealthy.

The Fourth Seal

The fourth seal is negative and seems to release the power for about one-fourth of the people on Earth to be destroyed.

The Fifth Seal

My understanding of the fifth seal is about the special call of this generation. We are the generation that will unite, and as a great spiritual army reclaim all that has been stolen by the forces of evil for world control.

Satan has foreknowledge, and he tried to destroy Moses and Jesus as babies because they were destined to be Saviors. Satan is doing it again by killing babies through abortion, knowing that this is the generation of the corporate body that will bring forth the Kingdom of God. We are the saviors of this generation.

Seven seals, to be released over a 42-month period, seem to me would probably be released about one every six months. So it appeared to me that the seventh seal, with all the terrible trumpet judgments, would probably have begun April 10, 1987, if my conclusions were correct. It is the sixth seal that is most important, however, and I will discuss that in the next section in more detail.

When the church is totally broken, we will come together into unity as that perfect man. At this point the church will receive the anointing that will break the yoke upon all Christians.

Isaiah 10:27

27. *And it shall come to pass in that day, that his burden shall be taken away from off thy shoulder, and his yoke from off thy neck, and the yoke shall be destroyed because of the anointing.*

When the church comes into unity, Isaiah 11:1-5 speaks of the Branch separate from the Rod of Jesse or the Vine. This is our church when we come into unity and there is a corporate anointing. It speaks to the body as a single person all of one mind and accord. This is that perfect man on the white horse that will go forth conquering in the name of the Lord. Zechariah speaks of the anointing given to the Branch when he prophesied to Zerubbabel, one of the olive branches in the fourth chapter of Zechariah. "Not by might, not by power, but by My Spirit," sayeth the Lord.

The Seventh Seal

Now let us look at the seventh seal and the events of April 10, 1987. I was told through a prophetic word that the vials were being poured forth that day. When I heard this, I went into prayer and further Bible study to understand what the Lord was telling me. I wondered how could this be on the day that I expected the seventh seal to be opened.

Revelation 5:8 states that the golden vials full of odors are the prayers of the saints. The odors in the vials are the prayers of the saints.

Now, as we look at Revelation 8:1, the opening of the seventh seal, there is silence IN HEAVEN for a half hour, and during this time we see in verse 3 that the prayers of the saints are offered upon the golden altar before the throne of God. Also during this half hour, the angels fill their censers with fire and there were voices, thunder, lightning, and earthquakes.

In 2 Peter 3:8, we are told one day with the Lord is as 1,000 years. Notice this half hour of silence is in Heaven and not upon the Earth. If this were a literal meaning, then the half hour of a 1,000-year day in Heaven would be 20 years and 83 days here on Earth.

God's prophetic clock sometimes stops and begins again. In Daniel's 70-week prophecy (Daniel 9:24-27), time stopped at the end of the sixty-ninth week, after 483 years of a prophecy that was to be fulfilled in 490 years. We have nearly a 2,000-year gap. The same thing is happening again after the seventh seal was opened. Of the 42-month period of the first half of the tribulation period, everything came to a stop after 36 months. The tribulation period didn't stop, however. Just the opposite occurred; it was extended. If the half hour in Heaven is a literal time period of a 1,000-year day, then the first half of the tribulation period is extended to 284 months and 23 days. Remember the illustration of the tire with the slow leak.

In other writings about the Book of Revelation, I go through the trumpet judgments, but for now I just want to point out one verse of scripture.

> *Revelation 11:15*
>
> 15. *And the seventh angel sounded: and there were great voices in heaven, saying, THE KINGDOMS OF THIS WORLD ARE BECOME THE KINGDOMS OF OUR LORD, AND OF HIS CHRIST; AND HE SHALL REIGN FOR EVER AND EVER.*

Remember this is the seventh trumpet, the very end of the first half of the tribulation period. This is the last trumpet. This is the time when the Lord comes with all of His saints and we meet Him in the air.

This surely is the beginning of the 1,000-year Millennial Kingdom of God on this Earth that begins after the first half of the tribulation.

REVELATION

In "Statement of My Present Understanding," I discussed what I believe to be happening through the breaking of the fifth seal.

The sixth seal is by far the most devastating, as well as the most important, to understanding the revelation of Biblical prophecy. Based upon what I believe I have heard and been taught, I will again attempt to put together a time line.

- On April 10, 1984, I was told the tribulation described in the Book of Revelation was beginning by the breaking of the first seal. The man on the white horse is the body of Christ coming together into unity to receive the anointing, break the yoke of Isaiah 10:27, and become the Branch of Isaiah 11:1-5. Each of the first six seals were opened in regular six-month intervals.
- The second seal opened on October 10, 1984.
- The third seal opened on April 10, 1985.
- The fourth seal opened on October 10, 1985.
- The fifth seal opened on April 10, 1986.
- The sixth seal opened on October 10, 1986.
- The seventh seal opened on April 10, 1987.

When the seventh seal was opened on April 10, 1987, a period of silence began in Heaven for one-half hour.

This was the beginning of a 42-month prophetic timetable where seven seals were released. They were released in a natural division of the 42 months, with one seal being broken every six months and each seal having a period of 42 months to be completed from the day the seal was broken.

The seventh seal was broken on April 10, 1987, which is the beginning of the devastating seven trumpet judgments, which are contained in and a part of the seventh seal.

The moment the seventh seal was opened, the prophetic clock, or timetable, was temporarily put on hold for a period of one-half hour in Heaven. The time is different in Heaven. We are told in 2 Peter 3:8 that one day to the Lord is as a 1,000 years. *One-half hour* in Heaven is a period of 20 years and 83 days upon this Earth. The prophetic timetable is scheduled to begin again in the summer of 2007. At that time there will be a continuation of the 42-month prophetic timetable with these times remaining:

First seal: 6 months remaining
Second seal: 12 months remaining
Third seal: 18 months remaining
Fourth seal: 24 months remaining
Fifth seal: 30 months remaining
Seventh seal: 42 months remaining containing the
                 7 trumpet judgments

The above statements are not speculations, but calculations based on literal interpretation of the Word of God.

The description of the man with a crown on his head

and an arrowless bow in his arms as he rides a white horse is a picture of the church under the anointing. The power is not in the arrow, or natural way, but is spiritual power under the crown of Jesus, the head. The words spoken to one of the olive branches were: *"Not by might, not by power, but by My Spirit."*

The prophetic overview of Revelation through the trumpet judgments is seen in Isaiah, Chapters 10 through 12.

We see the anti-christ described in Revelation 13. We also see another type of anti-christ, as a separate and different personality, described as the leader of the north countries as they invade Israel as part of the fulfillment of the sixth trumpet judgment of the seventh seal. This person is Gog, described in Ezekiel 38 and 39. So in this overview, Isaiah is speaking of the release of his people from Gog.

> *Isaiah 10:20-27*
> 20. *And it shall come to pass in that day that the remnant of Israel, and as such as are escaped of the house of Jacob, shall no more again stay upon him that smote them; but shall stay upon the Lord, the Holy One of Israel, in truth.*
> 21. *The remnant shall return, even the remnant of Jacob unto the mighty God.*
> 22. *For though thy people Israel be as the sand of the sea, yet a remnant of them shall return and the consumption decreed shall overflow with righteousness.*

In verse 23, it is *Israel,* and not Judah, that is described as many as the sand of the sea. These are the ten lost tribes now identified as the church of Jesus Christ that will be reunited with Judah.

The consumption decreed is a planned destruction of the people that will be stopped because of the overflow of righteousness. The Lord is going to turn it around and destroy the destroyer.

> 23. *For the Lord God of hosts shall make a consumption, even determined in the midst of the land.*

This is the devastation of the armies of Gog described in Ezekiel 38 and 39.

> 24. *Therefore, thus sayeth the Lord God of hosts, O my people that dwellest in Zion, be not afraid of the Assyrian: he shall smite thee with a rod and shall lift up a staff against thee after the manner of Egypt.*

This verse speaks of several things: [1] The people dwelling in Zion is Judah and not Israel, [2] Israel is dwelling among the north countries trying to return to the land of Israel, [3] Judah is being persecuted separately from Syria, [4] Syria seems to have Judah under siege.

> 25. *For yet a very little while and the indignation shall cease, and mine anger in their destruction.*
> 26. *And the Lord of hosts shall stir up a scourge for him according to the slaughter of Midian at the rock of Oreb: as his rod was upon the sea, so shall he lift it up after the manner of Egypt.*

The slaughter of Midian was where Gideon and his 300 blew horns, broke pitchers, and the armies of Midian destroyed themselves in confusion. This freed Israel from the bondage of Midian. Something like this is going to happen again. The invading forces are going to destroy themselves.

The last part of this verse describes Moses. Just as he raised his rod to part the Red Sea for the people of Israel to cross on dry land, Moses will do a similar thing to free his people again in another Exodus.

> 27. *And it shall come to pass in that day, that his burden shall be taken away from off thy shoulder, and his yoke off thy neck, and the yoke shall be destroyed because of the anointing.*

This describes the power of the anointing given to God's people when they become one as that perfect man.

All these verses are coming to a focal point. Verses 28 through 34 in Isaiah 10 continue to describe the invading route and position of Magog prior to the shaking of the Earth that causes the confusion where the invading armies destroy themselves. According to the sixth trumpet judgment, there are 200 million soldiers.

Jeremiah 23:5-8 states that at this time His Branch will be glorious, and they will no longer remember the Passover because the deliverance from these invading armies will be something greater to be celebrated.

The story and the sequence of events continue through Isaiah Chapters 11 and 12. According to Ezekiel 39:25-28, this is the event that brings Israel and Judah together again into unity as one people. With this unity of the body of

Christ and Judah, the Branch becomes fully developed. But the power is given to the Branch even before this to bring upon the anointing to make it happen, with all seven spirits of the Lord operating with His standard of the seven eyes upon one stone.

> *Isaiah 11:1-5*
> 1. *And there shall come forth a rod out of the stem of Jesse, and a Branch shall grow out of his roots.*
> 2. *And the spirit of the Lord shall rest upon him, the spirit of wisdom and understanding, the spirit of counsel and mite, the spirit of knowledge and of the fear of the Lord.*
> 3. *And shall make him of quick understanding in the fear of the Lord: and he shall not judge after the sight of his eyes, neither reprove after the hearing of his ears.*
> 4. *But with righteousness shall he judge the poor, and reprove with equity for the meek of the Earth with the rod of his mouth: and he shall smite the Earth with the rod of his mouth, and with the breath of his lips shall he slay the wicked.*
> 5. *And righteousness shall be the girdle of his loins, and faithfulness the girdle of his reigns.*

Isaiah 11, starting with verse 12, describes the gathering of his people out of the northern nations as they return to the land of Israel.

Isaiah 12 is a song of praise, much as the song of Moses is, just like the song they sung after being delivered at the parting of the Red Sea.

Before we continue into Revelation and the possibilities of the sixth seal, I want to address the phrase, THE LORD

OUR RIGHTEOUSNESS. In Jeremiah 33:16, this phrase is used in reference to Jerusalem and Judah, and does not address the Lord directly. Notice the word used here is "She" and not "He." Other similar meanings are found in Isaiah 45:24, 54:17, 61:3, and Jeremiah 51:10.

This seems to be a statement of praise, and it will be spoken by the people praising the Lord for what He is doing through them in all power and authority. This may be like saying, "I am not righteous. I am a sinner saved by grace. Anything righteous in me is due to the Lord. The Lord is my righteousness. The rallying point among God's people: THE LORD OUR RIGHTEOUSNESS."

Now, let us look at the trumpet judgments of the seventh seal to see the similarities of the plagues that were put upon Egypt to free the people. Rather than freeing the people just from the land of Egypt, this plague falls upon one-third of the Earth to free God's people.

This man, in the spirit of Moses, will stand before Gog and demand, "Set my people free." And this man, Gog, refuses.

First trumpet
All the green vegetation upon one-third of the Earth is destroyed by fire.

Second trumpet
All the water in one-third of the oceans is turned to blood.

Third trumpet

All fresh water is turned into wormwood on one-third of the Earth.

Fourth trumpet

The sun quits shining upon one-third of the Earth.

Fifth trumpet

The bottomless pit is opened up, and demons and devils are allowed to torment evil people upon one-third of the Earth.

At this point, Gog releases the people who come out of the north countries with all the silver and the gold.

Like Pharol of Egypt, Gog decides to destroy the people to take back his lost wealth and gain more. His invasion of Israel is the fulfillment of Ezekiel 38 and 39, as well as the sixth trumpet judgment.

We have skipped over the sixth seal judgment, and we will discuss it here before we get to the seventh trumpet judgment.

> *Revelation 6:12-17*
> 12. *And I beheld when he had opened the sixth seal, and lo there was a great earthquake, and the sun became black as sackcloth of hair, and the moon became as blood.*
> 13. *And the stars of heaven fell unto the Earth, even as a fig tree casteth her untimely figs, when she is shaken of a mighty wind.*

14. *And the heavens departed as a scroll when it is rolled together; and every mountain and island moved out of their places.*

15. *And the kings of the Earth and the great men, and the rich men, and the chief captains, and the mighty men, and every bond man, and every free man, hid themselves in the dens and in the rocks of the mountains.*

16. *And said to the mountains and rocks fall on us, and hide us from the face of him that siteth on the throne, and from the wrath of the Lamb.*

17. *For the great day of his wrath is come; and who shall be able to stand?*

At this point, I want to say the Lord has revealed some things to me about this, and I am drawing a few conclusions that seem right to me. This is a statement of my present understanding, and you may take it for whatever that may mean.

The sun becomes more than black—it disappears—and the Earth itself becomes black. It no longer rotates around the sun. It no longer exists. The planets in the solar system change their orbits and are rolled up like a scroll into a fairly tight ring of circles, with each one having a new orbit around the Earth. The Earth has now become the center of the universe because the Son of God has come to dwell upon the Earth, and we have the new Heavens and the new Earth.

The sixth seal is the return of Christ.

The prophetic timetable stopped with 36 months remaining to complete the sixth seal, and 42 months remaining for the seventh seal. When the prophetic clock begins again on June 24, 2007, the sixth and the seventh seal events will be happening together simultaneously. Now, with what we have learned, let's add to the mixture the seventh seal.

Revelation 8:5

5. *And the angel took the censer, and filled it with fire of the altar, and cast it into the Earth and there were voices and thunderings and lightnings and an earthquake.*

Voices, thundering, and lightnings—what do these indicate?

Revelation 4:5

5. *And out of the throne proceeded lightnings and thunderings and voices: and there were seven lamps of fire burning before the throne, which are the seven spirits of God.*

Is this the departure from Heaven of the Lord with His saints and angels coming back to Earth?

You be the judge. I have stated a case and a possibility.

Revelation 11:15

15. *And, the seventh angel sounded; and there were great voices in heaven, saying. The kingdoms of this world are become the Kingdoms of our Lord, and of his Christ; and He shall reign forever and ever.*

What Happened to the Ten Lost Tribes?

What could have happened to the ten lost tribes of Israel? Where are the ten lost tribes of Israel today? Again, we must look at the prophetic scriptures of the sure Word of God. History was written in advance for the answers.

Ezekiel 5:1-3

1. *And thou, son of man, take thee a sharp knife, take thee a barber's razor and cause it to pass over thine head and upon thy beard; then take thee balances to weigh, and divide the hair.*

2. *Thou shalt burn with fire a third part in the midst of the city, when the days of the siege are fulfilled; and thou shalt take a third part, and smite it with a knife; and a third part thou shalt scatter in the wind; and I will draw out a sword after them.*

3. *Thou shalt also take thereof a few in number and bind them in thy skirt.*

What does it mean when Ezekiel burns one-third of the hair in the midst of the city? It means that after the 390-year siege is over, it ends with one-third of the people being burned in the middle of the cities. And another one-third of the people will be slain by the sword as they try to escape the burning cities. Another one-third of the people will escape the flame and will escape the sword and will escape being chased by the sword. The few in number,

Chronology of the Prophets Before the Fall of Samaria 722/1 BC

PROPHET	APPROX. DATES	KINGS OF JUDAH	KINGS OF ISRAEL
Obadiah	845	Jehoram	Joram
Joel	835	Joash	Jehu
Jonah	782	Amaziah and Uzziah (corengency) Assyrian King: Shalmaneser IV	Jeroboam II
Hosea	760-720	Uzziah, Jotham, Ahaz, Hezekiah	Jeroboam II, Zechariah, Shallum, Menahem, Pekahiah, Pekah, Hoshea
Amos	760	Uzziah	Jeroboam II
Isaiah	739-685	Uzziah, Jotham, Ahaz, Hezekiah, Manasseh	Pekah, Hoshea
Micah	737-690	Jotham, Ahaz, Hezekiah	Pekah, Hoshea

Chronology of the Prophets After the Fall of Samaria 722/1 BC

PROPHET	APPROX. DATES	KINGS OF JUDAH	FOREIGN KINGS
Nahum	650	Manasseh	Assyria: Ashurbanipal
Zephaniah	640	Josiah	
Jeremiah	627-580	Josiah, Jehoahaz, Jehoiakim, Jehoiachin, Zedekiah Exile Governor: Gedaliah	Babylon: Nabopolassar, Nebuchadnezzar
Habakkuk	609	Jehoiakim	Babylon: Nabopolassar
Daniel	605-530	Jehoiakim, Jehoiachin, Zedekiah	Babylon: Nebuchadnezzar, Neriglissar, Labashi-marduk, Evil-Merodach, Nabonidas Medo-Persia: Cyrus, probably Cambyses
Ezekiel	593-570	Zedekiah	Babylon: Nebuchadnezzar
Haggai	520	Governor: Zerubbabel	Medo-Persia: Darius I
Zechariah	520*	Governor: Zerubbabel	Medo-Persia: Daruis I
Malachi	433	Governor: Nehemiah	Medo-Persia: Darius II

---

* It's possible Zechariah continued his ministry to approximately 485.

Dynasties of the Northern Kingdom

Date	King	Accession Accomplished	Father
I. 931-909	**DYNASTY OF JEROBOAM**		**22 YEARS**
931-910	Jeroboam	Chosen by people	Nebat
910-909	Nadab	Inherited	Jeroboam
II. 909-885	**DYNASTY OF BAASHA**		**24 YEARS**
909-886	Baasha	Assassination	Common
886-885	Elah	Inherited	Baasha
III. 885	**DYNASTY OF ZIMRI**		**7 DAYS**
885	Zimri	Assassination	Common
IV. 885-841	**DYNASTY OF OMRI**		**44 YEARS**
885-874	Omri	Declared by army	Common
874-853	Ahab	Inherited	Omri
853-852	Ahaziah	Inherited	Ahab
853-841	Jehoram	Inherited	Ahab
V. 841-752	**DYNASTY OF JEHU**		**89 YEARS**
841-814	Jehu	Assassination	Nimshi
814-798	Jehoahaz	Inherited	Jehu
798-782	Jehoash	Inherited	Jehoahaz
793-753	Jeroboam II	Inherited	Jehoash
753-752	Zechariah	Inherited	Jeroboam II
VI. 752	**DYNASTY OF SHALLUM**		**1 MONTH**
752	Shallum	Assassination	Jabesh
VII. 752-740	**DYNASTY OF MENAHEM**		**12 YEARS**
752-742	Menahem	Assassination	Gadi
742-740	Pekahiah	Inherited	Menahem
VIII. 752-732	**DYNASTY OF PEKAH**		**20 YEARS**
752-732	Pekah	Coup d'etat	Remaliah
IX. 732-722	**DYNASTY OF HOSHEA**		**10 YEARS**
732-722	Hosheah	Assassination	Elah

The Kings of Assyria

Ashur-uballit I	1354-1318	Shamsi-Adad V	824-810
Adad-nirari I	1318-1264	Adad-nirari III	810-782
Shalmaneser I	1264-1234	Shalmaneser IV	782-773
Tukulti-ninurta I	1234-1197	Ashur-dan III	773-754
Ashur-dan I	1179-1133	Ashur-nirari V	754-745
Tiglath-pileser I	1115-1076	Tiglath-pileser III	745-727
Ashur-rabi II	1012-972	Shalmaneser V	727-722
Ashur-resh-ishi II	972-967	Sargon II	721-705
Tiglath-pileser II	967-935	Sennacherib	704-681
Ashur-dan II	935-912	Esarhaddon	681-669
Adad-nirari II	912-889	Ashur-banipal	669-633
Tukulti-Ninurta I	889-884	Ashur-etil-ilani	633-622
Ashur-nasir-apal II	884-858	Sin-shur-ishkun	621-612
Shalmaneser III	858-824	Ashur-uballit	612-608

The Fall of Ninevah 612

The Fall of Haran 610

The Fall of Carchemish 605

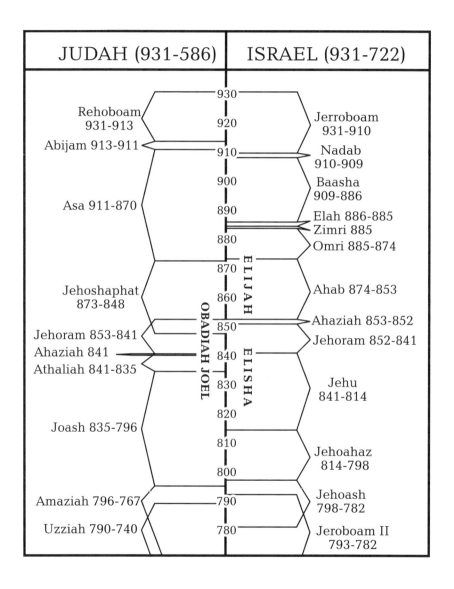

JUDAH (931-586)	ISRAEL (931-722)
Rehoboam 931-913	Jerroboam 931-910
Abijam 913-911	Nadab 910-909
Asa 911-870	Baasha 909-886
	Elah 886-885
	Zimri 885
	Omri 885-874
Jehoshaphat 873-848	Ahab 874-853
Jehoram 853-841	Ahaziah 853-852
Ahaziah 841	Jehoram 852-841
Athaliah 841-835	Jehu 841-814
Joash 835-796	Jehoahaz 814-798
Amaziah 796-767	Jehoash 798-782
Uzziah 790-740	Jeroboam II 793-782

ELIJAH
OBADIAH JOEL
ELISHA

930 920 910 900 890 880 870 860 850 840 830 820 810 800 790 780

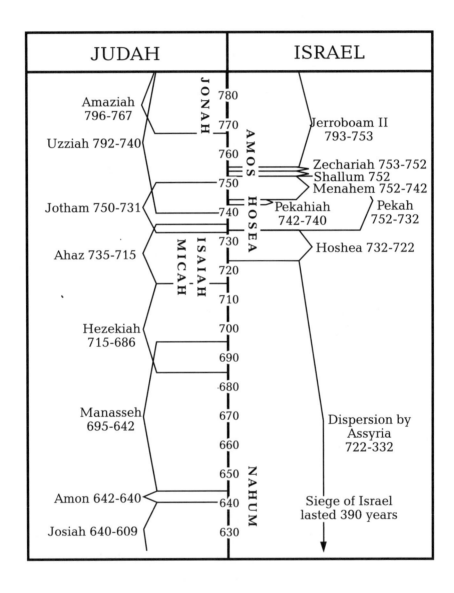

JUDAH	ISRAEL

Amaziah
796-767

Uzziah 792-740

Jotham 750-731

Ahaz 735-715

Hezekiah
715-686

Manasseh
695-642

Amon 642-640

Josiah 640-609

JONAH

AMOS

HOSEA

ISAIAH
MICAH

NAHUM

780
770
760
750
740
730
720
710
700
690
680
670
660
650
640
630

Jerroboam II
793-753

Zechariah 753-752
Shallum 752
Menahem 752-742

Pekahiah
742-740

Pekah
752-732

Hoshea 732-722

Dispersion by
Assyria
722-332

Siege of Israel
lasted 390 years

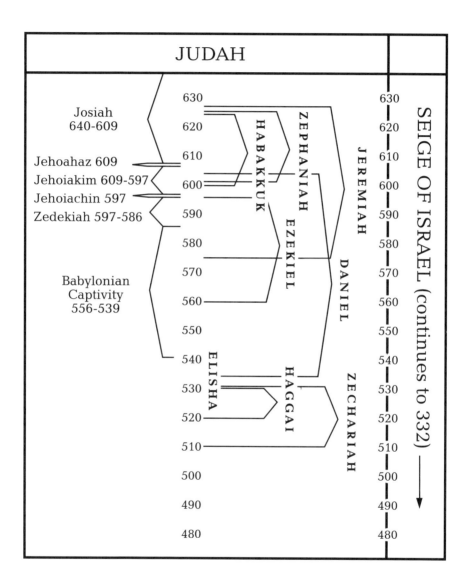

gathered into the hem of Ezekiel's skirt, represent the remnant few who become those that return to the land.

Who are the ten lost tribes today? How many may they be today? Archeological studies discovered in recent years claim that the actual number taken from the city of Samaria, and placed in bondage in 722 BC, was 27,290 people. Considering the fact that most of the people were farmers and sheep herders outside the cities, the total number of all the people in the countryside and in all the cities of all the ten tribes may have been several million people.

As an illustration of how this population may have expanded in 390 years, we can illustrate by the 70 people who went into Egypt with Joseph and his brothers. The Bible says that 430 years later, there were 600,000 adult men. If women and children are included, it rockets to a total of 3 million or more.

The point is that these people today may be so many that the stars of Heaven and the sand of the sea are a good illustration of their numbers. After 332 BC, all traces of the ten tribes of Israel cease to exist. This is due to the fact that over this length of time memories are lost. We don't know whom our ancestors were 645 years ago, the time between the separation of the tribes and when the siege ended. We don't know any of their values or beliefs or what their occupations were. These people are here on Earth and make up about 25% of the world population.

Ironically enough, around the same time that the ten tribe's historical records are lost, another group of people emerge from the area of the Euphrates River and migrate west. One of the areas they migrated to was Galatia, south of the Black Sea. They fought ferociously, burning Rome and fighting Caesar. The Celts, or Gauls, had many of the same characteristics as the people of the ten lost tribes.

Where one group of people disappears from world history, another group with similar characteristics develops in the very same area of the world. They had similar spiritual beliefs, such as atonement for sin, reincarnation, and the worship of sacred groves. As Israel sacrificed their children in fire, the Celtic peoples engaged in human sacrifice to their gods. These people make up the White Anglo-Saxon peoples of the world who fought their way into all European nations and settled Canada, America, and Australia.

Only the remnant held in the hem of Ezekiel's skirt will return. I don't know how many that will be, but I believe there is very strong evidence for these people being the ten lost tribes. None of this makes any difference spiritually, but the prophetic word of God is also the sure Word of God to be fulfilled in every detail.

JUDAH AND ISRAEL—
THE TEN LOST TRIBES

To understand where prophecy may be taking us as we try to decode the prophetic scriptures, we need to go back and review Old Testament scriptures and world history so that we can look correctly into future events. A main theme of Isaiah, Jeremiah, and Ezekiel is the regathering of Judah and Israel as one nation.

If we miss interpreting this correctly, it changes how we might foresee events described in future prophecies. We will be looking to see if we can answer the following questions:

1. Who is Israel as a people?
2. Who is Judah as a people?
3. Who are the people of the ten lost tribes?
4. Who is a Jew?
5. Who is an Israelite?
6. Who are you?

The earliest time in scripture that the word Jew is used is recorded in 2 Kings 16:6. This describes a war between Judah and the other ten tribes called Israel. The ten northern tribes that make up Israel were about to be overrun by Judah. The King of Israel asked the King of Syria to defeat the "Jews." Here we see the King of Israel calling the people of Judah *Jews*. So, we see the term *Jew* does not speak of the people of *Israel*, but only to the people of *Judah*.

Now we will examine the words that Moses spoke to all the tribes during the Exodus out of Egypt. The last speech that Moses made to his people before they crossed the Jordan into their Promised Land is a key to proper understanding.

Moses told the people of the blessings they would receive upon entering the Promised Land. Then he warned them and prophesied that if they turned away from the Lord, they would be scattered among all the nations of the world, and their numbers would be so many that they would be compared to the sand of the sea and the stars of Heaven.

Then Moses says: WHILE YOU ARE AMONG THE NATIONS OF THE WORLD, YOU WILL COME TO KNOW THE LORD AND WORSHIP HIM WITH ALL YOUR HEART; AND THEN THE LORD WILL CAUSE YOU TO RETURN TO YOUR LAND. They come to know the Lord while they are still among the nations of the world, before they return to their land.

Is that what you see happening in Israel today? The Bible says that Judah, or the Jews, will return before Israel returns to their land. Zechariah 12:7 states that the tents of Judah will be saved first so the glory of David and the inhabitants of Jerusalem don't magnify themselves against Judah.

What is the glory of David? None other than Jesus Christ and the followers of Jesus Christ. Judah was returned first so that the Christians wouldn't magnify themselves against Judah. Can you see what may have happened because many extremists over the past blamed the Jewish people for crucifying Christ?

To continue, we will look at Ezekiel's prophecies. We should remember that the true Word of God is absolutely sure, and although this is looking to a future event, it is sure and could very well be HISTORY WRITTEN IN ADVANCE.

> *Ezekiel 4:4-6*
> 4. *Lie thou also upon thy left side, and lay the iniquity of the house of Israel upon it: according to the number of the days that thou shalt lie upon it thou shalt bear their iniquity.*
> 5. *For I have laid upon thee the years of their iniquity, according to the number of the days; three hundred and ninety days: so shalt thou bear iniquity of the house of Israel.*
> 6. *And when thou hast accomplished them, lie again upon thy right side, and thou shalt bear the iniquity of the house of Judah forty days: I have appointed thee each day for a year. Ezekiel is told to lie on his left side for 390 days representing the years that Israel would be in captivity under siege.*

When did this captivity begin? It began in 722 BC when Assyria overthrew Israel and took them captive to the north in an area near the Euphrates River.

When did this 390-year siege end? It ended in 332 BC when Alexander the Great overthrew the Persian Empire.

When did Judah's captivity begin? It began 136 years

after Israel was taken into Assyria. Babylon did the same thing to Judah that Assyria did to Israel. They took them from their land to Babylon and held them captive.

How did Judah's captivity end? It ended when Cyrus, the king of Persia, threatened Babylon. This allowed Judah to become a self-governing autonomy within Babylon and ended their captivity after 40 years—in 546 BC. Judah did not return to their homeland for another ten years—in 536 BC. The last of the tribe of Judah returned with Ezra in 458 BC. Important points are that Judah was taken captive when only 136 years of Israel's siege was completed. They were taken to two different nations. Israel was taken to Assyria and Judah was taken to Babylon. When the last of Judah returned, Israel still had to serve 123 years of the sentenced punishment prophesied by Ezekiel.

We need to realize that reading scripture of this period, scriptures addressed to Jerusalem, the capital city of Judah, refers to the people of Judah. Prophecies to Benjamin refer to Judah because Benjamin became part of Judah when the ten northern tribes separated. On the other hand, scriptures that relate to Samaria, Israel's capital, relate to the ten tribes of Israel. Prophecies relating to Ephraim are also directed to the ten tribes because during that period Ephraim was a leading force.

Since Israel and Judah separated in 976 BC, they have never reunited. Even to this day, they are not together and don't recognize each other as independent nations. But Judah and Israel will be regathered as one nation in our generation.

THE LIVING CREATURES OF EZEKIEL'S VISION

Could Ezekiel's visions give us insight into this joint venture between Heaven and Earth that is taking shape as the church comes into unity as one body under the direction of the head, Jesus Christ? What was God showing this generation through these visions of the living creatures coming forth from the whirlwind? Has He given us understanding in this generation to show us what we can be, under submission to the head, as we let Christ take His proper position over His body? Why is the creature described in the tenth chapter of Ezekiel different than the creature Ezekiel describes in the first chapter of Ezekiel?

While I was asleep back in 1981, I suddenly awoke with a deep feeling that the Lord wanted me to open my Bible to Ezekiel's visions. As I started reading, a new understanding began forming in my mind, and I started writing my thoughts down. Over the months and years after this, additional thoughts and understanding came to me, and this will be a statement of my understanding of the meaning of these visions for this generation.

Ezekiel 1:4-10

4. *And I looked, and behold, a whirlwind came out of the north, a great cloud, and a fire enfolding itself, and a brightness was about it, and out of the midst thereof as the colour of amber, out of the midst of the fire.*

The whirlwind, cloud, brightness, color of amber, and the fire represent the glory around the throne of God.

> 5. *Also out of the midst thereof came the likeness of four living creatures.*

And this was their appearance; they had the likeness of a man. Even though they had four faces, wings, wheels, etc., their form still resembled the body of a man. Four living creatures full of eyes represent a corporate body rather than a single individual.

> 6. *And every one had four faces, and every one had four wings.*

There are four distinct personalities represented, and the wings are reference to the heavenly or spiritual part of this creature.

> 7. *And their feet were straight feet; and the soles of their feet was like the sole of a calf's foot; and they sparkled like the colour of burnished brass.*

The feet are the feet of a calf, and a calf is a baby ox. Being a baby signifies submission to the mother; the mother is the face of the ox personality. We will see that in scripture brass in many cases is a symbol of spirituality. Burnished brass is brass that must be continually polished for it to keep its shine—it loses its luster. The straightness of the feet represents a single direction—unwilling to change directions.

8. *And they had the hands of a man under the wings on their four sides; and they four had their faces and their wings.*

The wings represent the heavenly or spiritual, and the hands represent the earthly or the fleshly. The wings are for flying in the heavens, and the hands are for working on Earth. Together, we see a partnership or a joint venture between Heaven and Earth.

9. *Their wings were joined one to another, together.*

This is the determination and the single mindedness of the spiritual part of this creature to be obedient to the heavenly mission.

10. *As for the likeness of their faces, they four had the face of a man and the face of a lion on the right side; and they four had the face of an ox on the left side they also had the face of an eagle.*

The positions are important. Jesus sits at the right hand of the Father, and in this case the lion and the man are both on the side of honor. However, the lion has the most honored position of being placed above the man. In Revelation 5:5, Jesus is referred to as the Lion of the Tribe of Judah. In this vision, the Lion represents the Lord Jesus Christ.

* * *

In the last section, we saw that the Lion of the Tribe of Judah held the highest position of honor of the four personalities represented by the four faces of the four living creatures. The man is a symbol of the followers of Jesus Christ positioned with Him at the right hand of the Father in Heaven.

The right side of the living creature represents our position because of our faith and acceptance of the atonement of our sins through what Christ has done on the cross, and it is given to us as a free gift.

The left side represents the inner man, the soul, where the battle takes place between the things of the spirit and the lusts of the flesh. This is the battle between wills, either the Lord's perfect will or our self-will. We either worship and do the work of the Lord under His direction in total submission to the Lord as head, or we do the work of the Lord the way we think that the Lord may want us to do His work—in the righteousness of the flesh.

There are two personalities on the right, and only one personality on the left. Notice that the eagle is neither on the right, nor on the left. The eagle is out of position, as though he is waiting and watching for something to happen. The ox is the symbol for self-will or stubbornness of the flesh. All the other personalities of this living creature submit to the ox.

The self-will of the man that is trying to follow the Lord determines the direction of this living creature. As Jesus approached John the Baptist, who was preaching in the wilderness, John recognized Him because he saw the Holy

Spirit descending upon Jesus in the form of a dove. The dove is the symbol of the gifts of the spirit: meekness, patience, long-suffering, etc. This was the Holy Spirit's position in relationship to Christ, and His position of being the Lamb sacrificed on the cross as atonement for our sins. The Dove, or Holy Spirit, is grace, love, and integrity.

The eagle also represents the Spirit of Christ in His position of Lord of lords and King of kings as the head of His body. The eagle is the symbol of all the power and the authority of Christ that He wants to rule through on the Earth. That power and authority is not upon the Earth because of the ox's nature or self-will of serving God in the strength of the flesh. The ox does not let Christ rule through His position as head of the church.

> *Ezekiel 1:11-16*
> 11. *Thus were their faces; and their wings were stretched upward two wings of every creature were joined one to another, and two covered their bodies.*

Here we see the battle between the spirit and the flesh. The living creature is partly spiritual and partly fleshly, sometimes submitting to the spirit, symbolized by the wing's position of trying to fly, and at other times giving in to the flesh. Because the spirit never forces himself upon the flesh, the spirit submits to the will of the flesh and his wings are drawn from the heavenly spiritual position to covering the body—the earthly or fleshly position.

12. *And they went every one straight forward: whither the spirit was to go, they went; and they turned not when they went.*

The calf's feet are submitting to the ox and go straight. They turn neither to the right from the self-will of the ox nature—the flesh trying to do spiritual work—nor to the left. Although this spirit goes wherever the spirit leads, this is still the flesh because this is the spirit of man rather than the Spirit of God. The flesh, rather than the spirit, is controlling the soul.

13. *As for the likeness of the living creatures, their appearance was like the burning coals of fire, and like the appearance of lamps: it went up and down among the living creatures; and the fire was bright, and out of the fire went forth lightning.*

This is a picture of the glory of God within the body of Christ, the church. The lightning and the lamps are symbols of the light of the gospel of Jesus Christ. It is alive and well within the church, and goes up and down the body. We see this when the spirit manifests itself within the body with His presence in giving prophecies and healings, etc.

14. *And the living creatures ran and returned as the appearance of a flash of lightning. The spiritual effect of the church to the world is like a quick flash of lightning.*

The living creature is unable to maintain the glory and brightness in the world and returns to the body. The body is not standing in faith to the end of its mission. The spirit gives in to the flesh, and what starts out as spiritual ends up trying to do spiritual things through the power of the flesh.

> 15. *Now as I beheld the living creatures, behold one wheel upon the Earth by the living creatures, with his four faces.*

Wheels are used to move an object by having four wheels at the four corners with each wheel carrying an equal weight of the object.

The living creature has only one wheel upon the Earth. The body of Christ is accomplishing a work upon the Earth, but only one-fourth of the work available through proper alignment with the head.

> 16. *The appearance of the wheels and the work was like unto the colour of beryl: and they four had one likeness; and their work was as if it were a wheel in the middle of a wheel.*

The wheel within the wheel is another picture of the inner wheel being the guidance of the outer wheel that is a symbol of the work accomplished. When the wheel within the wheel gives the direction, the proper work is accomplished. It is not by might, not by power, but by the Spirit of the Lord.

The beryl is the color of the eighth level of the wall of the New Jerusalem that John saw as the bride ascending upon the Earth. Beryl is the color of new beginnings. We have seen a picture of the church the way it has been for 2000 years. As we continue, Ezekiel's visions will show us what we are about to become.

*   *   *

As we look at the living creatures, we discover there is a difference between the living creatures that Ezekiel describes in Chapter 1 and the living creature Ezekiel describes in Chapter 10.

Ezekiel's writings also give us insight to the time and sequence of events that I will also bring out as we study.

We can come to conclusions by interpreting what is meant by certain symbols and then putting precepts together and building upon these precepts. The following is the meaning and understanding, as I presently understand them, and is to be taken as a statement of my present understanding.

Symbols
1. Fire: Fire is a symbol of cleansing. Cleansing is achieved through judgment.
2. Cherubim: Cherubim are the plural of cherub. Cherubim are very special angels that surround the Holy of Holies and God's presence.
3. Wheels: The wheels full of eyes represent the work

being done by the body of Christ represented by the living creatures.

4. Living Creature: The living creatures are symbols of the body of Christ. I do not presently have an understanding why there are four living creatures. It may very well represent four different segments. One possibility may be that the Lord is reaching others besides Christians.

5. Eyes: Eyes are a symbol of enlightenment and represent those workers within the body of Christ.

6. Cloud: The cloud represents a manifestation of the Spirit of God.

7. Glory of God: The glory of God is different from the Spirit of God and is glorious visually in the conscience beyond description.

8. House: The house in these scriptures represents the Temple of God that will be built upon the Temple Square in Jerusalem.

The sequence and the reason for the events leading up to where we want to go in this study are important, and we need to start in the eighth chapter of Ezekiel. These were actual events that happened in Ezekiel's day and are also a prophetic look at future events. This is common throughout the scriptures.

Here we see that Ezekiel is sitting in his own house (Ezekiel 8:1). The Lord's appearance was as fire or judgment. He is lifted up between Earth and Heaven, and is shown Jerusalem. Ezekiel is shown all the abominations being committed and is told that it is the house of Judah committing these abominations (Ezekiel 8:17).

The abominations have filled the land with violence and have provoked the Lord to anger.

As we move into Ezekiel Chapter 9, we see a man dressed in linen. This man is instructed to seal all the people within Jerusalem who have a heart for God.

After the sealing, judgment falls upon men, women, and children.

*   *   *

It appears that the man dressed in linen who is instructed to scatter coals upon Jerusalem is one of the two witnesses, or one of the two olive Branches, Joshua or Zerubbabel. This judgment falls upon Jerusalem after the sealing of all those following the Lord.

Now we will examine the living creatures described in the tenth chapter of Ezekiel.

> *Ezekiel 10:1-14*
>
> 1. *Then I looked, and, behold, in the firmament that was above the head of the cherubim there appeared over them as it were a sapphire stone, as the appearance of the likeness of a throne.*

The site of these events begins at the very throne of God.

> 2. *And he spake unto the man clothed with linen, and said, Go in between the wheels, even under the cherub, and fill*

thine hand with coals of fire from between the cherubim,
and scatter them over the city, And he went in, in my sight.

This judgment authority is to be given to a man of this generation symbolized by Joshua, one of the olive Branches. The coals are gathered from among the cherubim in the Holy of Holies of God's throne.

3. *Now the cherubim stood on the right side of the house when the man went in; and the cloud filled the inner court.*

The scene is now upon the Earth at the rebuilt Temple in Jerusalem.

4. *Then the glory of the Lord went up from the cherub, and stood over the house and the house was filled with the cloud, and the court was filled with the brightness of the Lord's glory.*
5. *And the sound of the cherubim's wings was heard even to the outer court, as the voice of the Almighty God when he speaketh.*
6. *And it came to pass, that when he had commanded the man clothed with linen saying, Take fire from between the wheels, from between the cherubim; then he went in and stood beside the wheels.*
7. *And one cherub stretched forth his hand from between the cherubim unto the fire that was between the cherubim, and took thereof, and put it into the hands of him that was clothed with linen: who took it and went out.*

Here we see the fire of Judgment again, the second time being handed to the man dressed in linen where he takes the authority and stands beside the wheels, which represent the people of God.

> 8. *And there appeared in the cherubim the form of a man's hand under their wings.*

NOTICE THE DIFFERENCE: In the first chapter of Ezekiel, we saw hands under the wings of the living creature. Now we see hands under the wings of God's most honored angels.

> 9. *And when I looked, behold the four wheels by the cherubim, one wheel by one cherub and another wheel by another cherub; and the appearance of the wheels was as the colour of a beryl stone.*

The emphasis of four wheels, one by each cherub, seems to mean there were four cherubs and four wheels for each living creature. Here we see the color beryl described as a beryl stone instead of as it was in Chapter 1 as beryl only. This may signify that believers have become building stones of God's Temple of believers.

> 10. *And as from their appearances, they had one likeness as if a wheel had been in the midst of a wheel.*
> 11. *When they went they went upon their four sides; they turned not as they went, but to the place whither the head looked they followed it; they turned not as they went.*

They went upon their sides—this implies that they go by spiritual power and they go to wherever the head looks, but they don't go alone because the wording is that they *followed*.

> 12. *And their whole body, and their backs and their hands and their wings, and their wheels were full of eyes round about, even the wheels they four had.*

Here we see that perfect man with many more eyes. The entire body is full of eyes, not just the wheels and the wings.

> 13. *As for the wheels it was cried unto him in my hearing, O wheel.*

This wording implies marvelous wonderment.

> 14. *And everyone had four faces; the first face was the face of a cherub, and the second face was the face of a man and the third face was the face of a Lion, and the fourth face of an eagle.*

Take note: no longer is there any distinction between the left and right side. The ox is no longer present but is replaced by a most honored cherub. The eagle is now in his proper position. Now there is total and complete unity, so all the power manifested from the lion and the eagle are working through this living creature. Transformation has taken place.

Everyone who enters into progressive states must go from the caterpillar to the cocoon, then emerge from the cocoon into the butterfly. When that one is truly free, his heart's desire is to go back to the other caterpillars and explain metamorphosis to them. The witness to them is seeing the change in the one that had also been a caterpillar.

God created this creature, commonly known to all men, to reveal, when they had eyes to see, what could really happen to them.

BLUEPRINTS FOR THE KINGDOM

God is now setting up His Kingdom through His Son, Jesus Christ, to rule upon this Earth through His Branch to bring glory to Himself. The Kingdom is made up of God's people anointed with the power and authority to break the yoke of bondage that Satan has placed upon the world. The Lord, through His mighty Holy Spirit of power and authority, will give all instructions.

The Kingdom that we are about to enter will never be destroyed and will never be taken away from the people of the Lord. This is an everlasting Kingdom that will never pass away, but will stand forever. Daniel, the prophet of God, interpreted King Nebuchadnezzar's dream and wrote about the Kingdom coming forth in our day in Daniel 2:44, 45.

> *Daniel 2: 44, 45*
>
> 44. *And IN the days of these kings shall the God of heaven set up a kingdom, which shall never be destroyed: and the kingdom shall not be left to other people, but it will break in pieces and consume all these kingdoms, and it shall stand forever.*
>
> 45. *For as much as thou sawest that the stone was cut out of the mountain without hands, and that it brake in pieces the iron, the brass, the clay, the silver and the gold; the great God hath made known to the king what shall come to pass hereafter; and the dream is certain and the interpretation thereof sure.*

We are the generation bringing forth the stone cut out of the mountain without hands. This is not being done by or through the efforts of any man, but is being done by all the body that lets God work through spirit-led men and women—men and women who are totally submitted to the point where they can be under the control of God's Holy Spirit. The Kingdom is the body of Christ and not any church or denomination. This will be made up of people coming out of all faiths of the world, which includes Hindu, Moslem, and all the rest.

People throughout the world are seeking truth. All of us, to some degree, have been misled in some area of our faith. All will come through the death and resurrection of the cross. Many people have a yearning in their heart for truth and light. Many of them may not know exactly what to call that yearning in their hearts, but the Holy Spirit is Christ Himself speaking to their hearts. We are now going to learn the blueprints of how this will happen. The prophet, Zechariah, speaks about the structure of the working order of God's way.

> *Zechariah 3:7, 8, 9*
> 7. *Thus sayeth the Lord of Hosts; If thou wilt walk in my ways, and if thou wilt keep my charge, then thou shalt also judge my house, and shalt also keep my courts, and I will give thee places to walk among those that stand by.*
> 8. *Hear now, O Joshua the High priest, thou and thy fellows that sit before thee; for they are men wondered at: for, behold, I will bring forth my servant the BRANCH.*

Here is God's promise to those believers in the Messiah who are totally dedicated and submitted to Him. He will make them rulers in His Kingdom represented by the stone cut out of the mountain without hands. Joshua and those who sit before him are men wondered at because they have the seven spirits of God working that were given to the Branch. They have given themselves totally to God's purposes.

> 9. *For behold the stone that I have laid before Joshua; upon one stone will be seven eyes: behold I will engrave the graving thereof, sayeth the Lord of Hosts, and I will remove the iniquity of the land in one day.*

Here, we are given the structure and working principals for establishing the Kingdom of God on this Earth. The stone being placed before Joshua represents the entire Kingdom of God on this Earth.

It is my belief that inside this Kingdom of God on Earth will be lesser governing bodies very similar to what we have today, such as city, county, and state government within the federal government. The term "upon one stone" in verse 9 implies more than one stone the way it is phrased. We are going to see that there are two forms of government represented by two symbols of the olive branches. Joshua symbolizes the priestly government, and we will see that Zerubbabel represents the civil government.

Zechariah 4:6-10

6. *Then he answered and spake unto me, saying, This is the word of the Lord unto Zerubbabel, saying not by might nor by power, but by my spirit, sayeth the Lord of Hosts.*

7. *Who art thou, O Great Mountain? Before Zerubbabel thou shalt become a plain; and he shall bring forth the headstone thereof with shoutings, crying, Grace, grace, unto it.*

8. *Moreover the word of the Lord came unto me saying,*

9. *The hands of Zerubbabel have laid the foundation of this house; his hands shall also finish it; and thou shalt know that the Lord of Hosts hath sent me unto you.*

10. *For who hath despised the day of small things? For they shall rejoice, and shall see the plummet in the hand of Zerubbabel with those seven; they are the eyes of the Lord, which run to and fro through the whole Earth.*

The plummet represents the standard of the Lord's righteousness. The headstone is a symbol of the Kingdom of God. The mountain represents the world and obstacles placed before this generation in establishing the Kingdom. The Spirit of the Lord will remove them, and they will become as a plain. When the world sees this happening, many will turn their hearts to the Lord and will become a part of this great work.

*   *   *

We will see if it might be possible to read properly the blueprints for the body of Christ to structure itself in the building of the Kingdom of God. In the case where the stone is cut out of the mountain without hands that Daniel prophesied in Daniel 2:44, the mountain is the world and the stone is the body of Christ bringing forth the Kingdom of God. This seems to be a two-staged event:

1. The first stage is the believers of all churches, denominations, and religions recognize that Jesus is the savior of the world and there is a coming together into one body—a body of believers without labels or divisions.
2. The second stage is the operational structure. This is how we become the BRANCH, where there is no mountain or problem that cannot be removed. The words to Zerubbabel were: "Not by might, not by power, but by My Spirit, sayeth the Lord."

From the various uses of a stone being a symbol, we see the church as a stone in Daniel 2:44. We see Jesus as the chief cornerstone, and we see believers and individual stones making up the body of Christ. So the stone is cut out of the mountain without hands under the direction of the chief cornerstone, and the work is done through the body as directed by the head.

Maybe a pyramid will be a good example to illustrate the structure made of stone as well as an illustration of a plumbline. The chief cornerstone and the headstone of a pyramid are the same. Visualize in your mind the chief cornerstone at the top of a pyramid, but without any other structure—just resting there in space at exactly the right spot to build with the perfect plans and specifications for the entire structure.

From this point, the headstone can build a perfect structure. With the plumbline, we can put every stone in its perfect place. We can make sure every corner is exactly right, and we can even be sure every surface of the walls are perfectly smooth. This is an illustration of how the body of Christ is to become all of one mind and accord in perfect alignment with Jesus Christ, the chief cornerstone or headstone.

Now in your mind, visualize Jesus as that headstone in the structure of the building of the body of Christ. The plumbline coming from the Lord to form the corners and put every stone in order is spoken of as eyes by Zechariah. He says there will be "seven eyes upon one stone." Eyes are for seeing physically. To see spiritually, we need seers or prophets. The prophets in the past were the eyes that could see the light of the Holy Spirit and what the Lord wanted to tell His people.

Because we have been trying to serve God in a way that seemed right by the wisdom of the flesh, rather than by the inspiration and guidance of the Holy Spirit, we have missed a great deal of what the Lord wanted for the church. Many times, the Holy Spirit edifies and encourages, but He also chastises and corrects. When this happens, many people will not accept this as truth and may say, "That was not God speaking," and they will accuse the prophet of being a false prophet. Sometimes, what we hear is not what we want to hear but what we *need* to hear. Even though we may not like the words of correction, it is still the Lord speaking. If this word is not accepted, the Holy Spirit is grieved and prophesy ends within that body. God never forces His will upon anyone.

Today, there are few congregations where the Lord can speak freely to a submissive body eager to hear.

The Lord is going to set up a plumbline standard. The seven eyes upon one stone are seven prophets in a position of honor within every priestly authority. Joshua and the seven eyes upon one stone symbolize them. Every civil authority is symbolized by Zerubbabel and those seven men wondered at which were spoken of by Zechariah.

The line that we saw coming down from the very top of the headstone that keeps everything in perfect alignment with the will of God, is the ability to continually be under the guidance of the Lord by always hearing His direction through His seven prophets. This will be the plumbline in action. When decisions are to be made by the body, they are not to be made by the showing of hands. The decisions of a pastor or a deacon board of directors will be submitted to the seven prophets before implementing. These prophets will seek to hear from God to be sure that they are in alignment with the will of the Lord. By submitting to the Word of the Lord, we will always know that we are acting within the boundaries of God's will regarding every situation.

* * *

As we continue reading the blueprints for the body of Christ's structure of becoming fully submitted to the power and authority of Christ, we will go through the fourth chapter of Zechariah.

> *Zechariah 4:1-14*
> 1. *And the angel that talked with me came again, and waked me, as a man that is wakened out of his sleep.*
> 2. *And said unto me, what see'st thou? And I said, I have looked and behold, a candlestick-all of gold with a bowl upon the top of it, and his seven lamps there on, and seven pipes to the seven lamps, which are on the top thereof.*

To properly read this blueprint, we must understand what each item symbolizes or represents. We have the golden candlestick, a bowl, seven lamps, and seven pipes.

The Golden Lampstand:

In Revelation 1:2, we see seven golden candlesticks that represent the seven foundational churches where Christianity began. These seven churches were responsible for giving the light of God to the world, and this is represented in the seven candles.

The golden lampstand is only one, but it is a lampstand that raises up and supports seven lamps. The point I want to make is that the lampstand raises up the light, and seven lamps give much more light than seven candles.

The lamps are attached to the bowl holding the golden oil for the lamps, and together they are on top of the golden lampstand. The bowl that holds the golden oil and the seven lamps represents the Holy Spirit in power and authority, manifesting the seven spirits of the Lord, described in the first five verses of Isaiah 11.

The Seven Pipes:

The seven pipes are transporters of light and represent the Word of God being given through seven prophets, the seven eyes, on a continual basis, always an open line, never a busy signal. The Word is always flowing.

We have seven lamps giving the light of the Holy Spirit. Where is the light shining? Here we see seven pipes for seven lamps where all the light is compressed into a pipe.

This is like Laser Beam Technology where all the light is directed to a single spot, and it becomes great power. Where is the light going?

3. *And the olive trees by it, one upon the right side of the bowl and the other upon the left side thereof...The light is shining upon the two olive trees.*

4. *So I answered and spake to the angel that talked with me, saying, What are these, my lord?*

5. *Then the angel that talked with me answered and said unto me, Knowest thou not what these be? And I said, NO, my lord.*

I answered the question in the following verses through the anointing and the power of the plumbline.

6. *Then he answered and spake unto me saying, This is the word of the Lord unto Zerubbabel, saying, Not by might, nor by power, but by my spirit, sayeth the Lord of Hosts.*

7. *Who art thou, O great mountain? Before Zerubbabel, thou shalt become a plain; and he shall bring forth the headstone thereof with shouting and crying, Grace, grace unto it.*

This is the power that breaks the yoke that Satan has upon his people (Isaiah 10:27).

8. *Moreover, the word of the Lord came unto me, saying,*
9. *The hands of Zerubbabel have laid the foundation of this house; his hands shall also finish it; and thou shalt know the Lord of Hosts hath sent me unto you.*

Zerubbabel was part of building the Temple described in the Book of Haggai, but the prophecy is only partially fulfilled and is looking to the events of this generation also.

10. *For who hath despised the day of small things? For they shall rejoice, and shall see the plummet in the hand of Zerubbabel with those seven; they are the eyes of the Lord, which run to and fro through the whole Earth.*

The prophetic word is that Zerubbabel has laid the foundation, and he will finish it with those seven who are the eyes of the Lord. The eyes are the seers or prophets directing the work of building the Kingdom.

11. *Then answered I, and said unto him, What are these two olive trees upon the right side of the candlestick and upon the left side thereof?*

Now the terminology changes from a tree to a branch. The two individual branches represent Joshua and Zerubbabel individually, and the two pipes from them show the special anointing of the Holy Spirit to the two witnesses that stand before the whole Earth. The power flows out of themselves in power and authority to perform the acts described in Chapter 11 of Revelation about these two that stand before the Lord of the whole Earth.

> 12. *And I answered again, and said unto him, What be these two olive branches which through the two golden pipes empty the golden oil out of themselves?*
> 13. *And he answered me and said, Knowest thou not what these be? And I said, No my lord.*
> 14. *Then said he, These are the two anointed ones, that stand by the Lord of the whole Earth.*

The wording of the identification of the two witnesses in Revelation speak of the two olive trees and the two candlesticks standing before the God of the Earth (Revelation 11:4).

The wording of both the olive tree and the olive branch signifies power coming from the body of believers corporately, as well as the power and authority given to the two witnesses individually. *"Not by might, not by power, but by My Spirit, sayeth the Lord."*

THE TEMPLE: REBUILT FOR THE RETURN OF CHRIST

In the prophet Ezekiel's writings, the most was written about the rebuilding of the Temple on the Temple Mount in Jerusalem. Eight chapters are written about rebuilding the Temple and the redevelopment of the land of Israel. Why should there be so much written about the structure of this building? Let us see if we can find out some of the answers.

We will see connecting phrases and precepts to what we have previously discussed in discovering the four "living creatures." We will see connections to Zechariah's prophesies, a relationship to the anointed Branches, and even evidence of the return of Jesus Christ to the rebuilt Temple.

At the beginning, Ezekiel describes how the Lord again took him on a vision to a high mountain. Ezekiel was in Babylon, in captivity with Judah, when he was taken on a vision to the land of Israel and saw how the Temple would be built and wrote down the measurements for its construction.

Ezekiel 40:2, 3
2. *The visions of God brought me into the land of Israel and set me upon a very high mountain by which was a frame of a city on the south.*
3. *And he brought me thither, and behold, there was a man*

whose appearance was of brass with a line of flax in his
hand, and a measuring reed; and he stood in the gate.

Jerusalem is a city in the southern portion of the land of Israel. The Temple that Ezekiel saw was different than Solomon's Temple. Nothing is said about the altar of incense, nothing is said about the lampstands, and nothing is said about the Ark of the Covenant. We will see if there may be a reason for this.

Altar of Incense: we saw as the prayers of the saints as the smoke and the incense ascended up before God (Revelation 8:3, 4).

The Lampstand: held up the seven lamps that gave all their light to the two olive branches through the seven pipes (Zechariah 4:2).

The Ark of the Covenant: held the following tokens of promise:

1. The Ten Commandments
2. The Manna
3. Aaron's Rod that budded

The point we should consider is that upon the return of Christ to this Earth: Is there a need for the Ark of the Covenant? Everything held in the Ark of the Covenant is tokens of God's promises. When Christ returns, all of His promises will have been kept and fulfilled. The tokens of promise could be compared to a promissory note that has been paid. After it is paid, the note is destroyed because it is no longer in effect.

1. The Ten Commandments were fulfilled on the cross as Christ paid the price of our sins with His blood.
2. The Manna, the bread of life, will be fulfilled when the Word of the Lord goes forth from Jerusalem to the rest of the world on a daily basis, just as the water covers the sea.
3. The Lord, bringing forth His Branch in power and glory, will fulfill Aaron's Rod. The Rod will again have budded into new life as the Branch brings glory to the Lord.

Now let us take a close look at Ezekiel.

Ezekiel 43:1-2

1. *Afterwards he brought me to the gate, even the gate that looketh toward the east.*
2. *And, behold, the glory of the Lord of Israel came from the way of the east; and his voice was like the noise of many waters and the Earth shined with his glory.*

Is this not a picture of Jesus Christ entering the Temple that will soon be built upon the Temple Mount in Jerusalem? Is this the time of His Second Coming? Is this when He came in the clouds with all His saints, and we were raised up to meet Him and were changed in the twinkling of an eye?

Based upon Revelation 11:15, could this be the beginning of the 1,000-year Millennial Kingdom? Could this be after the seventh trumpet judgment in the middle of the seven-year tribulation period?

We will turn to Daniel to see if we can get some answers.

> *Daniel 7:13, 14*
> 13. *I saw in the night visions, and behold, one like the son of man came with the clouds of heaven and came to the ancient of days, and they brought him near before him.*
> 14. *And there was given him dominion, and glory, and a kingdom, that all people, nations, languages, should serve him: his dominion is an everlasting dominion, which shall not pass away, and his kingdom that which shall not be destroyed.*

Now we have another mystery. Who is the *ancient of days* who hands over the kingdom to Jesus? We will search to see who is referred to as the "ancient of days."

> *Isaiah 51:9*
> 9. *Awake, awake, put on strength, O arm of the Lord; awake, as in the ancient of days, in the generations of old, art thou not it that hath cut Rahab, and wounded the dragon. (The Lord brought the people out of Egypt, by Moses, whom he empowered as his stretched out arm [Exodus 6:6].)*

The above verse refers to Moses as the stretched out arm of the Lord. This verse is saying, "Wake up and put on faith, and work as you did in the ancient of days in the generation of Rahab when she was delivered from the destruction of Jericho as a result of her faith in the Lord." The wounding of the dragon refers to the wounding of Satan through the plagues and Exodus out of Egypt (Hebrews 11:31; Deuteronomy 4:34).

When Daniel saw Christ coming into his kingdom in glory, he met the "ancient of days."

Could Moses, as one of the two witnesses, fulfill this prophecy?

> *Ezekiel 43:3-7*
>
> 3. *And it was according to the vision which I saw, even according to the vision that I saw when I came to destroy the city, and the visions were like the visions that I saw by the river Che'bar. And I fell upon my face.*
> 4. *And the glory of the Lord came into the house by the way of the gate whose prospect is toward the east.*
> 5. *So the spirit took me up, and brought me into the inner court, and, behold, the glory of the Lord filled the house.*
> 6. *And I heard him (The Lord) speaking unto me out of the house and the man stood by me.*
> 7. *And he said unto me, son of man, the place of my throne, and the place of the soles of my feet, where I will dwell in the midst of the children of Israel forever, and my holy name, shall the house of Israel no more defile, their whoredom, nor by caresses of the Kings in high places.*

In these verses of Daniel, Isaiah, and Ezekiel, they show us a picture of the kingdom being given to the Lord by Moses, the ancient of days. We see the glory of the Lord entering into the Temple in Jerusalem. We see the Lord in the Temple speaking to Ezekiel, telling him that this is His throne and the place of the soles of His feet. The place where the Lord will dwell in the midst of His people, Israel, forever.

NEBUCHADNEZZAR'S DREAM

As we take a new look at Nebuchadnezzar's dream and Daniel's interpretation recorded in the second chapter of Daniel, verses 32 to 38, we are able to see other possibilities of how this may pertain to this generation.

Daniel 2:32-38

32. *This image's head was of fine gold, his breast and his arms of silver, his belly and thighs of brass.*
33. *His legs of iron, his feet part of iron and part of clay.*
34. *Thou sawest till that stone was cut out without hands which smote the image upon his feet that were of iron and clay, and brake them to pieces.*
35. *Then was the iron, the clay, the brass, the silver, and the gold, broken to pieces together, and become like the chaff of the summer threshing floor; and the wind carried them away, that no place was found for them: and the stone that smote the image became a great mountain, and filled the whole Earth.*
36. *This is the dream; and we will tell the interpretation thereof before the king.*
37. *Thou, O king, art a king of kings; for the God of heaven hath given thee a kingdom, power, and strength, and glory.*
38. *And where ever the children of men dwell, the beasts of the field and the fowls of the heaven hath he given into thine hand, and hath made thee ruler over them all, thou art the head of gold.*

Nebuchadnezzar was king of the Babylonian Empire. The Babylonian Empire existed between 625 BC and 539 BC.

This was the empire of gold.

In 539 BC, Cyrus reestablished this area into a larger kingdom, the Persian Empire. The Persian Empire was an extension and a reestablishment of the Babylonian Empire, so this should still be considered a part of the gold kingdom.

The Median Empire started the same year as the Babylonian Empire in 625 BC. The Median Empire bordered Babylon to the north and ended in 550 BC. So the kingdom of gold established by Nebuchadnezzar did not end with Babylon, but was kept intact under a different government.

If this is reasonable thinking that the kingdoms continued and only the controlling governments changed, the gold kingdom would extend from 625 BC to 332 BC. This period would represent the head of the image.

Alexander the Great overthrew the Persian Empire in 332 BC. Most Bible commentaries and Bible teachers state that this was one of the great kingdoms of the world and is the silver kingdom in this vision. I doubt that this is the proper meaning, due to the fact that this kingdom was a failure after only nine years. Alexander was surely a great conqueror, but his kingdom ended in failure upon his death when it was split between Alexander's generals.

Between the head and the shoulders is the neck. This may be a period between 332 BC and 27 BC. A period of struggling to establish territories as a result of the Celtic or Gaelic migration after the empire of their captors was overthrown by Alexander the Great in 332 BC. In the writing about the ten lost tribes, I showed strong evidence of these Celtic people being the ten tribes.

The Roman Empire, which we would have to call the silver kingdom, began in 27 BC and ended in 565 AD. The shoulders separate into two arms. The Roman Empire had two parts: the Western Roman Empire, consisting of the European nations as we know them today; and the Eastern Roman Empire, which was all the area around the Mediterranean Sea, consisting of such modern nations as Egypt, Israel, Jordan, Syria, Iraq, and Turkey.

Could this be the two arms of the vision? One represents the Western Roman Empire and the other the Eastern Roman Empire. The motivation of the Western Roman Empire was Christianity while the motivation of the Eastern Roman Empire was Islam.

Two dominant empires existed between 600 AD and 1400 AD. One was Christian; the other, Islam. Earlier, we saw that brass was the color representing those seeking God, even though they were doing so in their own strength in Ezekiel's vision of the living creatures.

Notice that the brass kingdom will rule the Earth. It appears that this may be an unfulfilled prophecy that may be fulfilled by the Branch in this generation. The brass becomes the two thighs—another separation.

The brass, or faith, movement of these two faiths continue as the legs of iron eventually become a part of the stone cut out of the mountain without hands.

From the 1400's until this day, we have seen the development of two separate areas in the world divided by faith.

The feet may represent stability, something to stand for or support, of all the nations making up these legs. Could the UN and NATO be organizations that try to hold up these kingdoms and let us walk in peace?

Everyone seems to agree that the ten toes represent the New World Order that is now being put together and is an attempt for the anti-christ to take over.

In taking another look at this vision and world history, I concluded with the following reasoning. The image is solid with no separations. Maybe this is a picture representing a continuous time period from the time of Nebuchadnezzar to the anti-christ. The shape in human form was a part of the proper discernment. Notice that the stone cut out of the mountain does not fall on the toes but upon the feet.

A conclusion that may be reached is that the anti-christ system tries to get established. But because of the power of the church coming into unity as a Branch, Satan's system is blocked in this generation. Babylon falls and we enter into the Millennial Kingdom. This puts the fulfillment of the 666-system back to be fulfilled after the 1,000 years.

And IN the days of these kings (Daniel 2:44). Since it doesn't say *after*, this could very well mean that the body of Christ is able to bind the power of Satan for 1,000 years through binding prayers of the entire body of Christ, in unity, all of one mind and accord.

BREASTPLATE OF JUDGMENT

The people God chose to live on Earth began with one man, who thereafter brought into being a household, which eventually turned into a nation. The one man was Abraham, the household was of Jacob, and the nation was Israel. When there was only one man, God appeared to him, giving him revelation and speaking to him. Later, when the children of Israel were delivered out of slavery and came under the name, authority, and discipline of the Lord, they became the nation of God.

The Bible shows us that at that time God changed the way of revelation to them. He no longer appeared or spoke to just one man as He formerly did. Instead, He adopted a new, special method by which to reveal Himself and speak to His people. The new method was the breastplate of judgment. Now, whenever problems or difficulties developed among God's people, they were to come to the Lord and ask for His guidance and revelation by means of the breastplate of judgment.

The breastplate of judgment was something the high priest wore whenever he went before God. It was firmly bound to the ephod, which the high priest alone wore. On this breastplate were four rows of precious stones. On these stones were written the names of the twelve tribes of Israel. When he entered into the presence of the Lord, he entered on behalf of the entire house of Israel because of the ephod with the twelve stones representing the twelve tribes.

Whenever the people of Israel were confronted with difficulties or unsolvable problems, the high priest would go before the Lord wearing the breastplate of judgment. Within the breastplate was found the urim and the thummim. Through the urim and thummim, the high priest was able to determine the Lord's will concerning the question at hand.

The way God revealed His will to His people in those days is similar to the way that He wants to reveal His will to the people of this generation. The method the Lord wants us to understand today is the principle of seven eyes upon one stone. When we were looking at Zechariah Chapter 4 and discerning what we called the blueprints for the Kingdom, we spoke of the seven eyes upon one stone (Zechariah 3:8, 9).

When the people of God come into unity as one body, the way of the Lord's revelation will change. At that time, He will reveal His will through the seven eyes.

Seven honored positions within any group of believers will be the office of the prophets. Seven elders of the church, who are totally submitted and wait upon the Lord to hear His voice, will take upon their shoulders the body before the Lord in the same way the priest took the burdens of the twelve tribes before the Lord with the breastplate of judgment. If we are to become the Branch and live according to God's standard, we need the breaking of the cross. Not only the seven holding the honored position of seers, or prophets, but every other person in the church needs to be broken as well. If we all learn this principle,

God will be able to speak and exercise His power and authority through us.

Authority in the scriptures is not based on position, but instead it is based on resurrected life. For example, the people of Israel recognized the authority of Aaron because they saw that Aaron's Rod budded. Authority in the body of Christ is based upon life, not position. The power and authority will come through Jesus Christ—the Root, the Vine—and will be ministered through His Branch.

> *Isaiah 11:10*
> 10. *And in that day there shall be a root of Jesse, which shall stand for an ensign of the people: to it shall the gentile seek; and his rest shall be glorious.*

JUDGMENT COMING

Aside from the work of creation, the Lord has not done any work greater than judgment. The first work He did was creation, and His last work is judgment. Without judgment, God's purpose of creation cannot be arrived at. So in His plan for mankind, judgment is constructive and not destructive.

After judgment, we are told that Christ will be with us. Through judgment, God sanctifies Himself. What I mean to say is: the way a crime is judged expresses the kind of person handing down the judgment. The judge of a court is honored according to the judgment he gives—the act of being fair according to the law, regardless of anything else.

Judgment causes us to know ourselves and exposes all hidden things. All things of the world will be exposed on the day of God's judgment. The day of judgment is God's great cleansing day. Our mistake is that when we think of judgment we think of punishment. But God takes no delight in punishing men. Both the ark and the flood came from God. The ark offered redemption, whereas the flood judged the world. The ark saved Noah, but the flood saved the world.

The Book of Revelation is the book of judgment that glides over the Millennial Kingdom, which is the 1,000 years that people on this Earth learn righteousness. This is the time of peace between the two judgments of the first three and one-half years of tribulation, and the second three and one-half years called the great tribulation.

Judgment is not only a burning fire. It is also the enlightening fire. Because of this light, men will hide in caves and call upon the mountains and rocks to cover them. In judgment, whatever is covered will be uncovered and will show the things which God has found in us.

When we look at judgment, we recognize whom God is. To know God as Lord is to know Him through the redemption of Christ Jesus. If we don't know God as Lord, we can only know Him as God, and knowing Him only as God is quite another thing. Through judgment, those not accepting Him as Lord will know the terror of God, and their worship will be in a different attitude from those worshipping Him as Lord.

Judgment is God's work in accomplishing His plan and purpose, and is both terrible and loving. Before the arrival of the trumpet judgments that we discussed in the writings on Revelation, Jesus was sent by His father to die on the cross. He provided the way of personal salvation for all.

The cross saves not by setting judgment aside—on the contrary, the cross itself is judgment. The judgment of the cross offers salvation. Salvation fulfills judgment, not by overcoming it, but by reaching the blood of Christ to go through it. The cross of Christ is the judgment for those who will believe.

When speaking of the judgment that will be manifested by the Lord through His Branch, we see restitution for all that has been taken from believers by the world.

Isaiah 11:4, 5

4. *But with righteousness shall he judge the poor, and reprove with equity for the meek of the Earth: and he shall smite the Earth with the rod of his mouth, and with the breath of his lips shall he slay the wicked.*

5. *And righteousness shall be the girdle of his loins and the girdle of his reigns.*

THE PLACE PREPARED
FOR SINNERS

Jesus spoke this parable to those who think they are righteous.

Luke 18:10-14

10. *Two men went up into the Temple to pray; the one a Pharisee, and the other a publican.*

11. *The Pharisee stood and prayed thus with himself, God I thank thee, that I am not as other men are, extortioners, unjust, adulterers, or even as this publican.*

12. *I fast twice in the week, I give tithes of all that I posses.*

13. *And the publican, standing afar off, would not lift up so much as his eyes unto heaven, but smote upon his breast, saying, God be merciful to me a sinner.*

14. *I tell you this man went down to his house justified rather than the other; for every one that exalteth himself shall be abased; and he that humbleth himself shall be exalted.*

The Lord says that two men go into the Temple to pray. One is a Pharisee, the best of men; the other, a publican, the worst of men. Surprisingly, the result of their prayers is that the worst, the publican, is justified whereas the best, the Pharisee, is condemned. The Lord Jesus announces that a good man goes to hell, but a bad man goes to Heaven.

We naturally reason that a good man goes to Heaven and a bad man goes to hell. But the Lord declares just the opposite. Everyone in Heaven, apart from the Lord Jesus, must be a sinner. In Heaven, you will not find or see a good man. All in Heaven are sinners, and a lot of good men go to hell.

If you declare yourself righteous and better than the average person, then according to the Word of the Lord Jesus, a good man may go to hell. But if you humble yourself and acknowledge yourself as sinful, you need not despair of not being worthy to be saved. For, according to Jesus, a bad man may go to Heaven.

Many deem themselves to be good and incorrectly conclude that they will be saved. Many are still trying to be good in order to be saved. They do not heed what the Lord Jesus has said, "Good men go to hell." The self-righteous Pharisee has already gone to hell. He serves as the prime example for all who would desire to be saved by doing good.

If anyone desires to be saved, he must acknowledge himself a helpless sinner.

He cannot save himself nor rely on himself in any way. Without humility, who will do this? Nothing under Heaven requires more humility than believing in the Lord Jesus as Savior. Self-exalted ones will never seek salvation by accepting the despised cross and thus will not be saved.

This Pharisee has already perished, and we should regard this as a divine warning. This man erred in his theory of salvation on two counts. First, he thought he needed to do good in order to be saved. Second, he deemed himself already good enough to be saved.

Ephesians 2:8, 9

8. *For by grace are ye saved through faith; and that not of yourselves. It is the gift of God.*

9. *Not of works, lest any man should boast. We are not saved by good works but* are *saved by believing in the grace of the Lord Jesus.*

Whether a person is saved or perishes is determined by his believing or not believing—by accepting or rejecting the salvation, which the Lord Jesus has accomplished on the cross. It is not determined by personal good or bad qualities. Our good deeds will never save us because we can never buy God's salvation with good deeds. The divine order is to be saved first and then do good.

In the days of Jesus, the Jews were under the rule of the Roman government. In the eyes of the Jews at this time, the most degraded, dirty, and sinful of all professions was to be a publican tax collector.

The Romans adopted the system of bidding for Jewish custom's revenue. The Roman government would decide how much tax must be collected in a certain place and then open it for bids. The publicans were those people who won the bids. They would deliver the amount of tax money they had bid to the government, but would charge the people above this for as much profit as possible. These publicans aided and abetted the foreign government in the oppression of their countrymen. They extorted money from their own people to profit themselves. Therefore, they were despised by society not only as outcasts, but also as the basest of men.

Yet the Lord Jesus says to us that the publican is the one who is justified, and that the bad one is the one who goes to Heaven. The publican, by his own admission, is a sinner.

Now I want to speak directly to those of you reading this. You may consider yourself unworthy to be saved and beyond redemption. But, praise the Lord, you can confess this to the Lord and be saved. Let me tell you: don't despair, and don't give up hope. Yes, you are a sinner for sure. But Jesus declares that sinners can go to Heaven. This is the gospel being presented to you.

Though you are a sinner, you may still have eternal life. In spite of your inability to save yourself, you may be saved. For there is salvation in the Lord Jesus. Come! Right now! Accept His salvation. This can be your prayer:

> *Lord Jesus, I am a sinner and cannot save myself. I, here and now, accept You into my heart as my Lord and Savior to be a part of Your Kingdom. I give You my life just as it is for whatever purpose You may have for it. Thank you, Lord Jesus, for dying on the cross for me. Thank you for forgiving all my sins and giving me eternal life. Amen.*

None but sinners are chosen for Heaven. Any saved person in this world must admit he is a sinner. If we could ask all who are in Heaven about their past credentials, all would say that they were sinners before. Heaven is inhabited with sinners saved by grace. It is a place *prepared* for sinners. This is the generation entering into the Kingdom of God, but being saved is not enough for the Kingdom. You become qualified to enter the *race* to the Kingdom.

THE RACE TO THE KINGDOM

In God's plan for man, He presents eternal life to sinners and presents the Kingdom to all that already have eternal life. We are shown the way to have eternal life. One needs to believe. But to enter the Kingdom, one is required to fulfill another condition.

Soon after a person is saved, he is set on a specific course for his life that lies ahead of him. The Christian life is like running a race, but this is not a race towards the goal of eternal life. In this race, only the person who has eternal life is qualified to run. The result of this race is that some of the participants will be crowned.

> *1 Corinthians 9:24, 25*
> 24. *Know ye not that they which run in a race run all, but one receiveth the prize? So run, that ye may obtain.*
> 25. *And every man that striveth for the mastery is temperate in all things. Now they do it to obtain a corruptible crown; but we are incorruptible.*

The crown represents the Kingdom and signifies reigning—having dominion and glory. To obtain the crown means to gain the Kingdom, to reign with the Lord Jesus, and to have dominion and glory. For a Christian to have eternal life is already a settled matter, but having the Kingdom depends on how that Christian runs the race.

As soon as a person is saved, God sets him on a course which leads straight to the Kingdom. His words, conduct, thoughts, and everything in his life are related to whether or not he may gain the Kingdom. We have all been placed as Christians on this course. But whether or not we win the Kingdom is a matter to be decided by our own selves.

Those that love the world and follow after the flesh are choosing between the kingdom of this world and the Kingdom of Heaven. They are possessors of eternal life only and not possessors of the Kingdom of God, having fully submitted to and trusting in the will of the Lord Jesus.

The Kingdom is the goal of our running the race. God gave us many witnesses in order to encourage us to live the life of faith.

> *Hebrews 12:1*
> 1. *Wherefore seeing also we are compassed about with a great cloud of witnesses, let us lay aside every weight, and the sin which doth so easily beset us, and let us run with patience the race that is set before us.*

The Kingdom before this generation is our goal. It depends how we run this race that will tell in the end of failure or success. He who overcomes will reign with Christ, but he that is defeated, even though he is saved, will have no part of the Kingdom of glory.

In running, two matters are absolutely important. One is to lay aside the weight. And the other is to put away sin. Sin hinders the race the most and disqualifies people from running. Sin is the trespassing of the rules, and he who breaks the rules is not allowed to run a race. He is ordered to the sidelines.

A weight may not be sin nor is it necessarily something bad, but it can easily entangle us. Anything that keeps us from running well or hinders our progress may be viewed as a weight.

> *Mark 4:19*
> 19. *And the cares of this world, and the deceitfulness of riches, and the lusts of other things entering in, choke the word, and becometh unfruitful.*

Here, the Lord Jesus says that the cares of the world, the deceitfulness of riches, and the lusts of other things entering in, choke the Word and it becomes unfruitful. Though riches are no sin, they nevertheless can hinder us. Those who desire to be rich cannot run well.

One's weight may be a deeply attached friend, a wanted position, or a much-desired new home. These may not be sins, yet they are able to slow down our speed.

We must also run the race with patience because the reward is not given at the start. Rather, it is given at the very *end* of the course. It is presented after the last lap of the race has been run.

We, of this generation, are well into the race and the goal is clearly seen.

RICH MAN THROUGH THE NEEDLE'S EYE

The Bible says it is easier for a camel to go through the eye of a needle than for a rich man to enter into the Kingdom of God. Is it impossible for a rich man to enter the Kingdom of God?

The meaning of the eye of the needle was different in that day than how we understand it today. The wall around Jerusalem had built into it a small opening that a man could enter the city through if he were caught outside the city after dark when all the gates were closed for protection. This small opening to re-enter the city was called *the eye of the needle*. For a camel to go through this small opening, it was necessary to unload the camel and have him go down on his knees to crawl through the small opening.

To answer this question, we will begin with an example of the young ruler in the eighteenth chapter of the Book of Luke. He was a man of good conduct, not a bad person before God. He had kept all the Commandments and had shown due respect to the Lord Jesus by calling Him a good teacher. And I'm sure the Lord Jesus considered him quite precious, for to meet such a person then, just as today, was quite rare. Looking upon him, Jesus loved him.

However, the Lord set down one requirement. If anyone desires to serve Him, he must be perfect. The Lord said, "If thou be perfect; one thing thou lackest." From this example, we can see that the Lord wants those who follow

Him, to follow Him perfectly, not lacking anything. He needed to sell all his property and distribute the proceeds to the poor, then the way would be clear for him to come and follow the Lord. Men may hoard wealth, but they cannot hoard happiness. As they accumulate wealth above their needs, they also accumulate trouble. Wealth and sorrow seem to always go together: to keep great wealth is to keep great sorrow. Those who are greedy of material things dwell with sorrow.

When the Lord stated to this rich young ruler that to be perfect and follow Him he should give his wealth to the poor, the rich young ruler turned and walked away. Having watched the young ruler depart sorrowfully, the Lord added a comment, "How shall they that have riches enter into the Kingdom of God?" The first question the young ruler asked was, "What must I do to have eternal life?" This is related, but not the same as entering into the Kingdom of God. As impossible as it is for a camel to enter through the eye of a needle, so it is equally impossible for a rich man to enter into the Kingdom of God. When Peter heard these words, he asked, "Then who can be saved?" Evidently, Peter wasn't comfortable about this.

The Lord answered in one sentence, and in this sentence lies the real issue. "The things, which are impossible with men, are possible with God." The Lord Himself acknowledged that what He was asking was humanly impossible.

God knows it is impossible for men to sell all that they have and give it to the poor. The young ruler could not abandon all, but God can do it. In other words, the Lord was prepared to give grace to the young man if he had only said, "O Lord, I cannot abandon my wealth, but give me grace. What is impossible with me is possible with you. Enable me to do what I am unable to do."

Man's failure is not due to his weakness, but to his not accepting God's strength. He cannot do it, but why not let God deliver him? *The things, which are impossible with men, are possible with God.*

Therefore, let us see that there is always a way, no matter how wealthy a man may be. If we can forsake all, as Peter did, we should thank God for that. But if we feel hesitant, as the young ruler did, then there is yet another way open to us. We merely need to bow our heads and say to the Lord, "I cannot," and He will undertake for us.

When God is at work, the camel passes through the needle's eye. With the rich young ruler, a camel walks around the needle's eye hesitantly and fails to go through. For the world, selling all is madness.

Let us learn not to be rooted in the world, but to hold things loosely—to be delivered from the things of the world is not a small matter. How many are the miserly people? How stingy are the people of the world? They are closed fisted, not only in big things, but in small things as well.

We, as God's people, must learn to be liberal toward others. Whether or not we actually sell our property and give to the poor, the sentiment is the same. We must be willing to share with others. Let us hold out nothing, even small things. We need to let all things go. If we obey this, God will not suffer us to have less. He will even give us more.

A Man of God
Must Be Obedient

The story recorded in 1 Kings 13 is a most tragic encounter of two men. It is about a man of God and an old prophet. These two men were both used by God, but one's end was most deplorable.

This old prophet in Bethel, a town in Israel, was a man who had been used by God in the past, but in his later life he was no longer a person the Lord could use. When God wished to warn Jeroboam of his sin in Bethel, He did not send the old prophet, who lived near King Jeroboam right in Bethel, to speak for Him. The Lord, instead, sent a man of God from the nation of Judah to speak for Him. This indicates that the old prophet was no longer useful to the Lord. The term *old* attached to the word *prophet* reflected neither his spiritual maturity, nor his rich spiritual experiences. Rather, it revealed the fact that he was spiritually aged and he no longer was fit for the Lord's service. In speaking to Jeroboam, the Lord could only use a man of God that was in communion with God. Communion is the basis of light from God, and the phrase "man of God" denotes such a one has communion with God. The old prophet had a spiritual history. He, at one time, was a prophet, but he lost his communion with the Lord. He became an old prophet that the Lord could no longer use.

The old prophet lived in Bethel where Jeroboam had

molded a calf as an idol for the people of Israel to worship and offer sacrifices to. Jeroboam ordained people as priests who were not Levites, and set the months and days for the burning of incense on the altar. Jeroboam did this because he was afraid the people would return to Jerusalem to offer sacrifices in the Holy Temple as prescribed by God.

A prophet can speak for God because he knows the mind of God. The old prophet saw all that Jeroboam had done. Yet the old prophet failed to recognize his sinful character, so the Lord had to send the man of God instead. When the Lord called upon the man of God to go to Bethel, He commanded him:

> *1 Kings 13:17*
> 17. *Thou shalt eat no bread nor drink water there, nor turn again to go by the way that thou camest.*

The man of God remembered this command, and he rejected the first invitation of the old prophet as well as the earlier invitation of the king. But the man of God was later deceived by the words of the old prophet when he lied to him by saying, "I also am a prophet as thou art; and an angel spake unto me by the word of Jehovah, saying, bring him with thee into thy house that he may eat and drink water."

The man of God reasoned that if the old man was a prophet, he certainly was more experienced than he. Therefore, he should obey him. So he returned with the old prophet and ate and drank at his house. The man of God violated the Lord's command due to the words of the old prophet. As a result, the man of God was slain by a lion after he left the old prophet's house.

At the beginning, the man of God was perfectly clear on the command of God. He became confused after hearing the claim that the old man was also a prophet of God. From this, we can derive a most important teaching: AFTER A SERVANT OF GOD HAS RECEIVED A CLEAR COMMAND FROM GOD, HE MUST NOT LISTEN TO ANY MAN, EVEN AN OLD PROPHET, IF THESE WORDS ARE DIFFERENT FROM WHAT GOD HAS COMMANDED.

THE GLORY OF JERUSALEM

Before the nations of the world become aware, God's people will come into unity and come forth as a great power. The Branch will come forth. It will appear as though it happened overnight. The corporate body of people from all regions and all nations will be as one, everyone letting Jesus Christ be Lord in every situation. We will be His International Branch of the Lion of Judah, all of one mind and accord, as that perfect man, as a nation of God.

Everyone will look to Jerusalem as their spiritual capital and will visit there often. Jerusalem will rejoice and be glad. All who love her and mourn for her will declare her their holy city—their capital city where we all will be a part of building a temple for our King, the King of kings, Jesus Christ.

God's people from all over the world will bring the wealth and glory from all nations of the world to dedicate it to the Lord on Mount Zion, God's Holy Mountain. All who come to Jerusalem will share in the wealth and glory brought into the city of peace. Everyone will be delighted, perfectly satisfied in the abundance of wealth.

The presence and glory of the Lord will be felt as joy in the heart of every person as they reach out to bless everyone they see. The glory of the Lord will be present upon God's Holy Mountain and will cover the entire city of Jerusalem. Everyone will be upholding one another in perfect love and peace.

Jerusalem will be the city known all over the world as the capital of God's glorious people. The city will make up His body of people from all nations. The leaders of Jerusalem will be men and women of responsibility and integrity, and will be known as people who judge righteously and give correct council on all matters. Jerusalem will be known as the righteous and faithful city where both Judah and Israel, along with many others, will declare, "We are the Lord's, we belong to Him, and He is our righteousness. We are His Branch."

The Lord will be exalted and raised up; for His endless love and righteousness will fill Jerusalem with correct judgment and equity for everyone. This standard of righteousness will be raised up to the world, and the people from every nation will be drawn near to His glorious city. People will say, "Light has come to Jerusalem through the King of kings, and His righteous Branch from all nations of the Earth."

As this light is centered upon Jerusalem, the Word of the Lord and the laws of righteousness will flow from Jerusalem like rivers of pure water dispelling darkness upon the entire Earth. Kings and rulers, as well as international business and financial leaders, will arise and come to the light upon Jerusalem to clean the streets, restore old buildings, and rebuild the walls of Jerusalem. They will bring their gold and their silver to be a part of building the Temple, and the beauty will become a wonder of the world. Where once there was brass, there will be gold. Where once there was iron, there will be silver. Where once there was wood, there will be brass.

Many nations will come and say, "Come with us up to the mountain of the Lord and He will teach us His ways, and we will walk in His paths and do as He says. The Word of the Lord and the laws of righteousness shall go forth from Jerusalem." Swords will be turned into plowshares as all military hardware and arms are converted to agricultural development and food production. The Earth will provide not only for the needs, but for the abundance of everyone. Peace will be among all nations, and world production will be at an all-time high. Ultimately, poverty will be eliminated upon the Earth.

The triumphant entry of the Lord Jesus into Jerusalem happened when the disciples did as He commanded them and brought forth the donkey, putting their coats on the donkey and setting Jesus upon it. Then a great multitude spread their garments in the path, and others cut down branches from the trees and spread them before Him. Then the multitude cried, saying, "Hosanna to the son of David. Blessed is he that cometh in the name of the Lord; Hosanna in the highest." Then all the people of Jerusalem were moved in the wonderment, saying, "Who is this?"

One day soon, I believe there will be another day where the people will say in wonderment, "Who are all of these people of the Lord entering into Jerusalem?" I'm sure there will again be palm trees honoring the King of kings and the Lord of lords as His Branch comes forth, and Judah and Israel again become one nation. This will be a glorious day for the land when this triumphant entry into Jerusalem of the body of Christ occurs.

THE KEYS TO THE KINGDOM

Now is the time to take the keys to the kingdom and enter the Kingdom of God. We are the chosen generation.

> *Matthew 11:12*
> 12. *And from the days of John the Baptist until the new kingdom of heaven suffereth violence, and the violent take it by force.*

Just as the children of Israel fought their way into the Promised Land, we, of this generation, are to battle our way spiritually into the Kingdom of God. Jesus spoke unto Peter.

> *Matthew 16:15-18*
> 15. *He said unto him, But whom say, ye that I am?*
> 16. *And Simon Peter answered and said, Thou art the Christ, the son of the living God.*
> 17. *And Jesus answered and said unto him, blessed art thou, Simon Bar Jona: for flesh and blood hath not revealed it unto thee, but my father, which is in heaven.*
> 18. *And I say also unto thee, that thou art Peter, and upon this rock I will build my church; and the gates of hell shall not prevail against it.*

The church is the body of Christ, and Jesus is speaking to the body of Christ today as an individual body, all of one mind and accord. The body was built upon the knowledge revealed to Peter. Peter said Jesus was the

Christ, the Son of the living God.

The weapons to bring forth this generation are the power and authority given to the body of Christ when they abide in Christ by submitting the Holy Spirit.

We have three weapons that may be used as the Spirit of the Lord is leading us.

1. We have the power and the authority of the name of Jesus Christ.
2. We have the power and the authority of the blood of Jesus Christ.
3. We have the power and the authority of the Word of God.

We have the power to bind specific events from happening or we may change the results. We may speak and pronounce miracles and healings without any limits, all according to the will of God. The limit of magnitude will be expanded according to the total power of all those praying of one accord in Christ Jesus.

Matthew 16:19
19. *And I will give unto thee [the body of Christ] the keys of the kingdom of heaven: and whatsoever thou shalt bind on Earth shall be bound in heaven and whatsoever thou shalt loose on Earth shall be loosed in heaven.*

After Jesus was tempted by the devil, He returned in the power of the spirit into Galilee. In Nazareth, He went into the synagogue and began reading from the Book of Isaiah. Jesus preached good tidings and proclaimed liberty to the captives and opened the prison to them that are bound by passing all the power and authority given to Him by the Father. The Branch can do nothing without abiding in the Vine.

> *John 15:55*
> 55. *I am the vine, ye are the branches; he that abideth in me and I in him, the same bringeth forth much fruit: for without me ye can do nothing.*

But, on the other hand, being fully submitted to the Lord is power.

> *John 15:77*
> 77. *If ye abide in me, and my words abide in you, ye shall ask what ye will and it shall be done unto you.*

Now, we will have a better understanding of the significance of what Jesus read in the sixty-first chapter of Isaiah and why He quit where He did.

> *Isaiah 61:1-2*
> 1. *The spirit of the Lord is upon me, because the Lord hath anointed me to preach good tidings unto the meek; he hath sent me to bind up the broken hearted, to proclaim liberty to the captives, and the opening of prison to them that are bound;*
> 2. *To proclaim the acceptable year of the Lord . . .*

Jesus then quit reading.

Luke 4:20-21

20. *And he closed the book, and he gave it again to the minister, and sat down. And the eyes of all them that were in the synagogue were fastened on him.*

21. *And he began to say unto them, this day is this scripture fulfilled in your ears. Jesus fulfilled the scripture that He read.*

Notice that Jesus quit reading in the middle of a sentence. The reason Jesus stopped where He did was because the rest of Isaiah, Chapter 61, will be fulfilled by the body of Jesus Christ, empowered with the Spirit of Jesus Christ—the keys to the Kingdom. Isaiah 61 continues by describing the mission of the Branch in bringing forth the Kingdom of God. This will not be done personally by our efforts—but will be done as we allow Christ to operate through us as empty vessels, fully submitted to the Lord. Now we will read the rest of the sentence in Isaiah 61:2:

Isaiah 61:2 (cont)

2. . . . *the day of vengeance of our God; to comfort all that mourn.*

We, as the body of Christ, His Branch, are to bring forth the Kingdom of God through the anointing given to us as we become fully submitted and led by the spirit.

Isaiah 10:27

27. *And it shall come to pass in that day, that his burden shall be taken away from off thy shoulder, and his yoke from off thy neck, and the yoke shall be destroyed because of the anointing.*

Isaiah 11:1-4

1. *And there shall come forth [Jesus] a rod out of the stem of Jesse, and a Branch, [believers with the keys to the kingdom] shall grow out of his [Jesus's] roots.*

2. *And the spirit of the Lord shall rest upon [the body, the branch] him, the spirit of wisdom and understanding, the spirit of counsel and might, the spirit of knowledge and of the fear of the Lord*

3. *And shall make him [Branch, body in one accord] of quick understanding, in the fear of the Lord: and he shall not judge after the sight of his eyes neither reprove after the hearing of his ears.*

4. *But with righteousness shall he [Branch] judge the poor, and reprove with equity for the meek of the Earth: and he [Branch] shall smite the Earth with the rod of his mouth, and with the breath of his lips shall he slay the wicked.*

The Lord gave the power and authority of the body of Christ to Peter with the keys to the Kingdom of Heaven in Luke 16:18-19. He gave the anointing and power to His body, the Branch, in Isaiah 10:27 and Isaiah 11:1-5. He confirmed it again in John 15:1-16, and He commissioned us for this work in John 17:18. Before we can do this work, the body of Christ must come into unity behind Jesus Christ. We all must be fully submitted. We must wait upon the Lord, and move only when and where He directs us to move. The power and authority are moving and acting under the direction, power, and authority of the one sending us. Then we all may say with authority, "We come in the name of our Lord Jesus Christ." This work is the work of an army, the army of God. Each one of us needs to be properly equipped under the anointing.

Ephesians 6:10-17

10. *Finally my brethren, be strong in the Lord, and in the power of his might.*

11. *Put on the whole armor of God, that you may be able to stand against the wiles of the devil.*

12. *For we wrestle not against flesh and blood, but against the rulers of darkness of this world, against spiritual wickedness in high places.*

13. *Wherefore take unto you the whole armor of God, that ye may be able to withstand in the evil day, and having done all stand.*

14. *Stand therefore, having your loins girt about with truth, and having on the breastplate of righteousness.*

15. *And your feet shod with the preparation of the Gospel of peace.*

16. *Above all, taking the shield of faith, wherewith ye shall be able to quench all the fiery darts of the wicked.*

17. *And take the helmet of salvation and the sword of the spirit, which is the word of God. We have the keys to the Kingdom of Heaven.*

We have the keys to bring forth the Kingdom of God upon the Earth. The Lord is now revealing the mystery.

Ephesians 1:9-10

9. *Having made known unto us the mystery of his will, according to his good pleasure which he hath purposed in himself.*

10. *That in the dispensation of the fullness of times he might gather together in one all things in Christ, both which are in heaven and which are on Earth; even in him.*

We, as the body of Christ, have the power of the stone. The power to build the house of God, stone by stone. As individual stones, we are responsible, each one of us, to use the key God has given each of us. As you read this next verse, take this as a personal message and a calling to you, giving you all the power and authority in Heaven.

Matthew 16:19

19. *Soon I will give unto thee the keys of the kingdom of heaven: and whatsoever thou shalt bind on Earth shall be bound in heaven: and whatsoever thou shalt loose on Earth shall be loosed in heaven.*

THE KEY TO UNDERSTANDING WHAT THE KEYS TO THE KINGDOM REALLY ARE, the Lord says, "I will give you the keys to the Kingdom." The Lord explains the power of the keys. The key is the power and the anointing given to each member of the body—the power to bind and loosen the powers on Earth, the power of the principalities, and the powers of Heaven. We have the keys to the Kingdom, the power to bind or release all the powers of Heaven or Earth.

This is not an individual power to bind all the powers upon Earth or in Heaven. This is power given to each person to bind or release the powers of his life and purpose, in taking upon himself the anointing given to carry out his individual purpose or calling of God. Believers all over the Earth have these powers.

This power is increased as people join together as

groups to pray and agree together. The problem today is that there are many individual groups separating themselves because of some label or specific doctrine that is emphasized. These divisions leave a lot of room for dissension and disputes that take away our prayer power because of disunity.

By coming together, stone upon stone, the spiritual Temple is being structured, and the corporate anointing to become God's Branch is taking place.

Budding of the Fig Tree

As we look at the prophecies that Jesus gave in the twenty-fourth chapter of Matthew, we see that the "Budding of the Fig Tree" will be fulfilled by the revelation of the Branch. In turn, that will be fulfilled when the body of Christ comes into unity as a perfect man and fulfills the reuniting of Judah and Israel.

As Jesus stood outside the Temple Square in Jerusalem, He prophesied to the disciples about the destruction of the Temple that they stood near. This prophecy was fulfilled with the destruction of the Temple in 70 AD.

Later, upon the Mount of Olives, His disciples came to Him and asked when these things would happen and then asked, "What shall be the sign of thy coming and the end of the world?"

Jesus answered the disciples by telling them of those that would come in His name, yet deceiving many. He spoke of all the wars to come and the famines and pestilence. He described the holocaust of the tribulation period and how the angels would gather His elect from one end of Heaven to another.

In all this, Jesus answered the question about the signs of His coming, but had not answered the question of when this would happen. This part of the question was answered in a parable of a fig tree.

Matthew 24:32-34
32. Jesus then said, "Now learn a parable of the fig tree;

when this BRANCH is yet tender, and putteth forth leaves,
you know that summer is nigh;

33. *So likewise ye, when ye shall see all these things, know that*
it is near, even at the doors.

34. *Verily I say unto you, "This generation shall not pass, till*
all these things be fulfilled."

Here, Jesus is speaking of a great sign that will be a sign to the generation just before He comes again to the Earth with all the saints with Him. His elect gathered from the ends of Heaven.

For a deeper understanding of the sign of the fig tree and its meaning, let us examine closely the tokens that were placed in the Ark of the Covenant. The sign of the rainbow is a token of promise (Genesis 9:13). God Himself became a token of promise to Moses (Genesis 17:11). The blood is the token of promise of the Passover (Exodus 12:13). Aaron's Rod was a sign against the rebels (Exodus 17:10). A token is a sign of a promise (Psalms 86:17).

What were the tokens of promises placed in the Ark of the Covenant? Why were these tokens placed in the Ark of the Covenant?

The Ark of the Covenant:

In fulfilling the ordinances of God's covenant with the children of Israel, there was made a tabernacle and in the first area were the candlestick and the table and the showbread. This area was called the sanctuary. Then there was a veil and the tabernacle called the Holiest of all or the Holy of Holies. Inside was the golden censer and this Ark overlaid with gold.

Inside the Ark was the golden pot, which had placed inside of it: manna, the Rod of Aaron's that budded, and the Ten Commandments.

The meaning and the fulfillment of these tokens placed in the Ark of the Covenant are the following:

The Ten Commandments: Jesus fulfilled the Ten Commandments when He was crucified on a dead tree for the atonement of sin.

The Rod of Aaron: The token of the fig tree will be fulfilled when the dead rod shoots forth into its Branch— when the Lord brings the body of Christ into unity as the anointed Branch of the Lord's planting.

The Manna: The manna hidden in the Ark of the Covenant will be fulfilled when the Word of the Lord is given out daily over the Earth from Jerusalem. The Word of the Lord must go forth from Jerusalem.

Many have correctly said that the fig tree is a sign to the nation of Israel. Scripture indeed does use a fig tree for a sign to the nation of Israel. THE FIG TREE STANDS FOR THE RETURN OF ISRAEL AND JUDAH TOGETHER AGAIN AS THE BRANCH OF THE LION OF JUDAH.

THE LIFE OF THE BRANCH

Truth does not refer to the words spoken about Jesus. It is Christ Himself who is truth. The way in which God gives is Christ, the truth God gives is Christ, and the life which God gives is Christ. Christ is our way, Christ is our truth, and Christ is our life.

God has not given us a method. He gives His own Son to us. Is Christ your way and is Christ your method? Or is Christianity only a way and a method? Doctrine and work are the way of death. The Lord is life; this life is effortless. THIS LIFE IS EFFORTLESS; THIS LIFE IS CHRIST HIMSELF. Life flows naturally into work, but work is never a substitute for life.

If there is life, there will not be the slightest need for our own doing—that life will naturally flow. If Christ is not life, we have to do all the work. But if He is life, then we do not need to struggle. Life is more profound than thought. It is deeper than emotion. Once we meet it, we are instantly quickened within. This quickening is the something within called life.

Knowing Christ requires a spiritual knowing and seeing within. Such seeing and knowing is the life of Christ within us. God gave His son Jesus to us. He is our way, He is our truth, and He is our life. Aside from Jesus Christ, there is no way, there is no truth, and there is no life. In God, there is nothing apart from Christ Jesus. All that God is, Christ is included. Christ is included in all that God is. People do not receive the power of God because they do not know who God is. The power of miracles and great works are of the Lord. Christ Himself is our substance. Christ is that miracle within us. We have not received the gift, but we *have* received the gift-giver.

We first receive the being of Christ Jesus, and then we receive the manifestation of His power in the form of having the manifestation. Jesus is the resurrection and the life. Without Christ, there is no resurrection. Resurrection is the manifestation of the substance or life, which is Christ Jesus. He is not only the life-giver, He is the life. He is the life given as well as the giver of life. Death is not able to hold Christ Jesus. Therefore, He is called life. Life is, therefore, not outside of Christ; it is Christ Himself.

Jesus is the resurrection and the life that was put to death, and yet is alive forever. In the power of the resurrection, there always remains the sign of death. In the resurrection of Christ, there was left the imprint of nails in His hands and the spear in His side. He bears the imprint of His death, yet He is alive. Alive is new, resurrected life. The sign of the resurrected life bears the imprint of death.

Our lives are judged by nothing if there is the imprint of death upon our pride. If there is the imprint of death upon our eloquence, if there is the imprint of death upon our cleverness and all our talents, then resurrection and the cross are inseparable—the cross eliminates self. In the power of a risen one, there is the sign of death. He is able to work, but he dares not rely on himself. He can do many deeds, yet he has lost that touch of pride and self-assurance, and his own strength has turned into weakness. Self has been eliminated by the cross and is unable to rise again because it is lost in death. Sometimes what was lost in the death of self is regained in Christ.

A BRANCH, when cut off from a willow tree, appears dead. But when the branch is planted in the Earth, it grows again in renewed life. The new shoot of the BRANCH of the Lord—the new life—comes forth. The trademark of God's BRANCH is His own body of Christ in resurrected power from death to become His INTERNATIONAL BRANCH OF THE LION OF JUDAH.

Come Under The Anointing

We must wake up from our sleep. This is the time to turn to the Lord. Come forth in power under the anointing. The Lord has made His Spirit available to you under the power and authority of His anointed Branch. The Spirit will be upon you as the Lord's man-child, but the Branch first must abide in the Vine in perfect unity, all of one mind and accord.

Stand up, sons and daughters of God; for He is calling you for a special purpose. He will empower you with His Spirit to stand as that perfect man before the nations and proclaim the Word of the Lord unto them. The Lord wants to place His anointing upon you. This anointing will break all bonds and every yoke that has held you down.

Every hindrance of every kind will be removed, and the mountains will become plains under the power of your anointing. The Lord is speaking and you must listen. He wants His people to step forth in His power and authority. Did He not say that you would be the head and not the tail? The Lord is asking you to step forth, and He will place Himself under your command to fulfill everything that He has spoken. But this takes faith and trust in His Word to stand unto the end on His Word, regardless of circumstances and how it may look.

He will provide a way where there is no way. The Lord is going to do mighty things through His people, even though they don't believe or accept it at this time.

The Kingdom of God is before you. We are to bring it forth in the name of Jesus. He has placed the Kingdom upon our shoulders; His people must bring it forth in His name, in the name of Jesus Christ. This is not to be done by the natural power of man, but by the power of the Spirit of the Lord.

Faith and obedience will lead to total submission to His authority and power, and He is then able to channel through us. He will lead us all upon the path that He has chosen for us; He has a narrow path for each individual to walk upon. He is able to keep you, and if you have the will, He will.

No one will be able to keep you from the path He has chosen for you. Trust the Lord to make you pillars that can be counted upon. None of you will go in your own strength. All, who wait patiently upon the Lord, will be made strong in the house that the Lord builds. A way will be opened, and you will know when to step out. Keep your eyes upon our Savior, your Redeemer, Jesus Christ. Look to no one else. Don't look back. Look only to the future. Don't even look to your own understanding. Put your faith and trust in the Lord, and every mountain will be made into a plain. The Lord is trusting you and me, His people, to do a mighty work.

We can and will trust Him. This will be like a trust fund arrangement that will bring all things that anyone needs. Everyone will discover what the Lord has placed for them.

The position the Lord has chosen for each one will fit no one else, and every individual plan the Lord has devised will be carried out by the mighty hand of God.

The wisdom and boldness of the Lord are for the taking and will be given to each one. With guidance through the power, His Spirit will keep everyone in perfect step. The Lord has ordained you and has chosen you all for a special work of His doing.

All those that are lowly and meek will be brought to a place where the Lord can speak and lead them through a prophet. Everyone will enter into a covenant to do only the Lord's will. The fruits and gifts of the Holy Spirit will be upon those the Lord has chosen; and we will all walk together, talk together, and uphold one another.

God's people are called from the lowly, but He will exalt them and they will not be ashamed. His people are the servants of mankind who will be lifted up. However, the proud and uplifted hand will be drawn back.

The Lord's people are blessed, as He has counted each one of us worthy that places Him in the realm of trust, faith, hope, and charity. Each one is to follow the leading of his heart and not his mind.

Anyone who leans on the Lord for understanding will be shown the way.

*   *   *

Many will be touched and follow after the Lord's overcomers, but others will want to slay those chosen of the Lord. The Lord will protect them and give them power over their enemy by the blood of Christ and having no fear of death. They will be honored by the Lord and will give honor back to the Lord. Each one will know that it is the Lord's conquest.

All direction will be given by the Lord with explicit instructions that will never vary from His written words in the Holy Bible. The scriptures are to be checked regarding all things spoken through a prophet. Even through a prophet, the Lord will never vary from His written Word. God's words are pure and they shall be adhered to.

The battle is not really ours, but the Lord's.

All the Lord needs are His people to be as empty vessels that He can move around at His will. If we totally submit and honor the Lord, not even a thought will come contrary to the thoughts of the Lord. The Lord will hedge each one in and plant them solidly in the spirit with His grace. The Lord's hand is upon each one, and all His power over the Earth will direct Him.

Directions for the job the Lord is sending each one will be given one day at a time.

Every morning we are to arise, praise the Lord, glorify His name, and see the works of the Lord. There will be no mistakes; for He, the Lord, will do it.

All that the Lord uses have to be in strict obedience, or correction will come. The Lord dwells among His people and will guide them. But not listening to the Lord shall cause a heavy heart to ascend upon His people. *All that the Lord uses have to be in strict obedience, or correction will come.* All that love God's Word will understand and know what He says and know what He means.

Following the Lord is a fine line that many cannot adhere to.

If God's people hear His voice, He will lead them. But a rebellious spirit is worse than witchcraft. All things are created by God and are for the benefit of the Lord's people. They will praise Him and thank Him for the things He has laid before them. The path God has chosen for each person is laid out clearly. It may be rough at times and some may come against us, but don't be discouraged. Your faith will make you the overcomer.

We will be the overcomers, and all that follow after the overcomers of the Lord will be rewarded. The Lord has many things ahead for each one of us. Remember the Lord's time may not be your time, and your time is not His time. All things will be stopped if they come against God's time. The Lord will do even more through you, but the present well has to be filled first. When the job is done, look for another duty the Lord has for you.

Each person has a job the Lord has chosen for him, but he must not step out on his own—this will bring confusion. The path will be cleared for each one by waiting and listening.

God will deal with each person and each situation in His own way. Only then will all obstacles be removed.

Keep your heart and mind focused upon the Lord, and you will do well and stay upon the correct path. Think things through, trusting the Lord to show you the correct way.

Each one is to walk day by day and walk in peace.

Even the words you speak will be prepared by the Lord.

The Lord has sent you, and your enemies will bow before you. They will not come against you as they think, but will recede and draw back. No one is to retrace his steps—that is the past and you have already covered that ground once. Don't consider the thoughts and plans of others, but rely only upon your heart. Let no one say to you that God has told him to tell you. The Lord himself will speak to you. Be obedient to the Lord's Word. Don't get confused about His Word. God's Word is a living Word. It is the same yesterday, today, and tomorrow. Check everything with the Bible. Then only believe and receive the word of faith.

*   *   *

Let nothing catch anyone unaware. Listen, and all things will be revealed by the Lord. Do not look at things as they appear to be. Rather, look at each person and each situation through the spiritual eyes of that still, small voice: the hearing and seeing of your heart.

Each person coming to you will be held accountable to the Lord for every word that he speaks. In times of trouble, many come with emotional words.

When this happens, stay on an even keel, still walking and talking to the Lord in faith.

Do not go or commit to anything without full understanding.

Don't let anyone control you in any way. You are on a

path provided by the Lord. Don't humble yourself to anyone's self-desire; for you are a child of the King. If any problem arises, be not afraid. The waters will part for you. The Lord has His angels that control everything about you.

Whenever you feel troubled, think upon the Lord. Think upon the Lord and the answers will come. Through the Spirit of the Lord, you will receive strength, power, and light. All things that the Lord speaks to any of His people will be according to the recorded Word of God in the Bible. Sift every thought with the Word of God to discern what He has spoken. All things spoken in the name of the Lord shall be adhered to. The fruit of the Vine crushed under His feet and His robe covered with blood are vengeance that can come upon the people.

Many who have accepted the Lord have not fully trusted upon His name.

Trust no one; for they may appear righteous and still be deceiving. The devil has power over those who will be deceived, but he has no power to deceive God's people. The Lord will stand against him. The Holy Spirit is our guide, our director. The Lord is always with us in spirit. You will receive instructions, and His will shall be carried out.

He wants people to give their wills and desires over to Him, so that He may rule through them and use their bodies to do His will on Earth. The Lord said, "Did not My Father work in the Old Testament? Did I not work in the New Testament, and does not the Holy Spirit now work upon the Earth?" Be strong, listen to no man, but only unto the Lord and prove everything by His Word. The Word was spirit preached, spirit written, and the books are closed.

Be assured that all who follow after the Lord in His perfect will by totally submitting their own wills, will always be led upon the right path. At times, this path is not easy, but always know that there is a reason and that the Lord will see you through all trials.

The valleys are deep and treacherous, but the Lord made a way. Those who walk with the Lord shall be preserved and nothing shall harm them. Walk in faith; for through the Lord endurance will be given to His people. Lift your voice in praise to the Lord for the victory that is to be won. Put on the whole armor of God, and let the weak say, "He is strong."

A battle must be fought before a victory, and we are in a battle for the Lord's Kingdom.

The battle will be fought by the saints of God, and they will prevail. Let the weak be overtaken through the strength of the Lord and put the enemy down. The gift of God is that all things shall be accomplished through the Lord's power and strength. Even if some arms have to be lifted up, as Moses's were lifted, lift them up and hold your hand high. The strength is not of you, but it is of the Lord.

If the Lord sends you, then you shall go; and if the Lord says stop, you will stop. Directions will be given to you and you only. It is the Lord, not those about you, that directs your path.

Be cautious and watch and pray always.

Many thoughts can enter the human mind that are not

of the Lord; and because of this, many people can be misguided. The heart belongs to the Lord, not the mind. The mind can trick many people. When you speak, listen to the things that testify of the heart by the spirit of grace. This is a mystery that the Lord has given His people, that they should understand and cast out thoughts that are not of Him.

*   *   *

The scriptures will not be changed, so listen to every word. The words will be imbedded in the Lord's people. For He is the resurrection and the life, and they will live by this Word. The fullness of time is now, and the Lord's people will be filled and know that the Lord Jesus is the God of Heaven and Earth. The Lord does not promise His people an easy walk. Did they not condemn Him as He walked upon this Earth? Shall you not also be condemned? Did they not speak of Him as a winebibber and a glutton?

And shall they not you also? The servant is not above his master. All the sons of God shall listen to the Spirit that gives utterance. The utterance speaks to the Lord, and He said He would answer. It shall not be tampered with, and neither shall it be cast out of His churches.

The letter of the law shall not prevail. His children have the law written within, and they will obey. He will not cushion His people. They shall hear Him face to face and will know that the words spoken will have power and are of the Spirit of the Lord.

It is an easy thing to walk with the Lord when you have walked in obedience, but disobedience shall be corrected with a rod of iron. If they walk with the Lord, He will answer with love, mercy, and kindness. If they abide in the Vine and He abides in the Branches, they can bear fruit. They will pluck, and they will eat in plenty and multiply.

As the tree shoots forth fruit, is not this seed replanted and does not another tree grow? He said this is the sowing of the Word. He has given you a picture.

All of you will counsel many through words that the Lord speaks through you. Have no confidence in fleshly understanding. It is what is revealed in your heart that gives life. It is only through the Lord that they will be satisfied.

No one will lead God's people whom He has not placed there. Many shall be brought in. They shall all hear, and they shall all know. The Lord provokes no one to anger. His people shall be meek and through love shall touch many. What the Lord puts before you will unfold from day to day, and you shall see the blessings of the Lord.

Your Special Assignment

You have a special duty that you were created to do that no other person on Earth can do. No other person in all creation was created in God's love to do what He wants *you* to do. I am speaking individually to everyone that may be directed by the Holy Spirit to read this, but the work is corporately for the entire body to accomplish.

Each one of us must find our position, place, and duty. We are a stone being formed out of a mountain without hands. In other words, mankind has no control over what is being done by the Lord. Right from the beginning, the human race was created to share His kingdom, to share His love.

No matter who you are or where you are, the Lord needs you to be what He created you to be. *This life in the flesh is for the purpose of testing every person's free choice, and we have to live by the decisions and choices we make.* However, even in spite of making the wrong choices sometimes, He still wants to use us. By free choice, we must experience the rebirth of our spiritual selves to have a personal relationship with God in order to be a part of this important Kingdom work.

The Lord has a free gift for every human being on this Earth, but everyone must reach out and accept it. It is no more complicated than that. Once you receive this gift, it's yours, forever. The Bible says that God's gifts are given without repentance. This means that it will never be taken away from you. The moment you receive this gift, you have eternal life. All of your sins are forgiven.

The Lord wants to use you, even if you haven't yet received the gift of salvation. But until you belong to the Lord, you are not qualified to do any work for the Lord. So the first step you can do right now is making this your prayer. Ask Jesus into your heart by saying:

Lord Jesus, I confess I am a sinner. I know that you died on the cross for me. Come into my heart now! Live my life for me and make me what You want me to be. I thank you for saving me and giving me eternal life. Give me the will to want to be a part of Your Kingdom work and make me an overcomer. Amen.

This is how we enter into the Kingdom work—by letting Jesus be the head. Let Jesus be your Lord.

Let Him have your will to make of you whatever He wants you to be. His plan for your life is a perfect plan.

Being saved and entering into the Kingdom are two separate matters. We may have eternal life by accepting Jesus as Savior, but we still may not be a part of the Kingdom. By accepting Christ we don't enter into the Kingdom, but we become *qualified* to enter into the Kingdom.

We enter the Kingdom by dying to our self—our own ego. When we are able to give up our will to do the Lord's will, we become qualified for Kingdom work and we will be a part of the Kingdom. We will be kings and priests unto the Lord.

Moses and Elijah! Come Forth!

The following series of writings are based upon scripture and what I believe the Lord has revealed to me prophetically. This is my understanding as to the proper meaning and the proper dividing of the Word of God. This is an interpretation of a series of compiled Biblical verses. In other words, it is a statement of my present understanding. It is written in a way that reflects my interpretations of how the Lord may speak to Moses and Elijah.

Moses and Elijah, come forth! I have put My Spirit upon you to bring forth My body, My man-child, My International Branch of the Lion of Judah. Rise up, My sons; for I have anointed you for this purpose. You will stand before My people and proclaim My words unto them. The bonds will be broken from My people when they see the great anointing that I have placed upon you.

Step forth, My sons, under My power and My authority. Remember this, My sons, did not I say that I have placed Myself under the command of My people to do all that I have said? And did I not say command ye the Lord? *(Revelation 12; Isaiah 10:27; Psalm 89:20; Isaiah 45:11).*

Step forth, My sons, the Kingdom of the Lord is before you! You are to bring it forth in the name of Jesus. The Kingdom has been placed upon your shoulders to be brought forth by the Spirit and power of the Lord working through you *(Isaiah 51:4, 5, 9-11)*.

You have totally submitted yourselves to My will. I have become the captain of your souls. I have given you the will to do My will. I have given you the mind of Christ and I say to you, "My sons, Thy will be done by Me, and My will be done through you. This is our joint venture! Total submission brings forth total power, and this power is in My Word spoken through you."

My Word has again become flesh in you. My people have yearned and waited for this day. The world is waiting for My arms to come forth. I have sworn by My right hand and the arm of My strength. I will no longer give the wealth and glory to the unjust *(Isaiah 63:12, 11:10)*.

Go forth and go through. Go through the gates and prepare the way of My people. Lift up a standard for the people. Set a sign before them. I will bring them into the nations of Europe, the United States, and Canada. My people will respond to My words that you speak, and they will be a witness giving a testimony to the nations of the world. And the nations will respond by bringing their wealth to Jerusalem upon My Holy Mountain *(Isaiah 11:10)*.

Blow ye the trumpet in Zion and sound the alarm on My Holy Mountain. Call together a solemn assembly. Gather the congregation. My Spirit is upon you to lift up the brokenhearted. You will open up all the prisons and proclaim liberty to the captives *(Joel 2)*.

Before the nations realize, My Spirit, My Word spoken through you will bring all My people into unity as a great army. All My people will look to Me in total submission and power. I will lead My people upon a highway of holiness. The mountains will become a plain and the crooked places will be made straight for My people.

This is My anointed Branch, My body, coming together in total submission to Me and submitting to one another through Me. My people and My man-child, through whom I am able to reclaim this Earth to our original plan, together, we will righteously judge the Earth. Every knee shall bow before Me and My people. The kings and priests of God will rule the kingdoms of this Earth *(Isaiah 11:1, 45:23; Revelation 12)*.

The time for Me to righteously judge My people upon the Earth has come. Through this judgment, My holy name will be known among My people and the heathen shall know that I am the Lord. All those who trust and put their hope in Me will be as trees planted by the waters.

A Branch, whose roots feed from the river of life, is My glorious BRANCH. My Branch will go through the great shaking of the heavens and the Earth and the sea. Soon, everything upon the Earth will shake and My people will be gathered together. The nations will be shaken, and their wealth and glory will be given and distributed to My people— the meek and lowly upon the Earth *(Haggai 2:4-9)*.

I will overthrow the governments and powers of the nations. Their strength will be broken, and their police forces and armies will panic and riot. They will turn their weapons upon their own friends, upon their neighbors, and even upon their own families *(Isaiah 41:11)*.

Violence will rise up with great wickedness of the entire Earth. But the righteous will remain unshaken. The violence will pass right over them, just as it did at the Exodus out of Egypt. But the wicked will be taken. The sword will be in the streets, and pestilence and great famines will devour all dwelling in unrighteousness *(Daniel 11:40).*

Many of My people will come out, repent of their evil ways, and escape. They will dwell in the mountains, hiding in caves, turning from their sins, and looking to Me. They will feel the shame and will humble themselves, even shaving the hair from their heads and dressing in sackcloth. The shame of the past will show upon their faces *(Jeremiah 16:16).*

People who have escaped the terror of the riots in the streets of all cities upon the Earth will throw all their wealth, all their money, all their jewelry, silver, and gold into the streets of all cities. They will see that in the day of the Lord's wrath all their personal wealth offered no protection or satisfaction. They will see that the wealth was the stumbling block that caused their iniquities *(Isaiah 60:6-9).*

From among all this tribulation upon the Earth will rise My people. A person in one city, or three or four from another city, will hear the voice of the Lord and refuse to react to circumstances. Instead, they will follow that still, small voice and move forward in faith. These people submit and look totally to Me for everything.

At first, they will seem to be few with no power. But soon they become an army, an army who lets Me, the Lord thy God, lead them. And we together break in pieces and consume all the governments of the world *(Daniel 2:44, 45).*

The stone cut out of the mountain without hands, the overcomers, the man-child, the BRANCH, the International BRANCH of the Lion of Judah—this is My Branch in total submission to Me, in unity, acting as a single person, everyone operating through the mind of Christ *(Isaiah 11:1-5).*

My man on the white horse, My body, with My crown and My signet ring, I give to thee My Branch. They will go throughout the entire Earth in total unity and perfect precision, overtaking kingdoms and establishing the Kingdom of God in the name of Jesus Christ. "This will not be done by the power or might of men, but will be done by My Spirit, sayeth the Lord" *(Revelation 6:2; Haggai 2:23; Zechariah 4:6).*

*   *   *

My sons, in that day when My people who have escaped out of the world look to Me, they will see My anointing upon you to bring My people into unity as a righteous army of God. The Branch of My planting *(Isaiah 10:27, 11:1-5).*

Everything that happens upon the Earth is under My control. But being a just God, I am submitting Myself to My people, who are part of all My movements, allowing the Holy Spirit to use them as channels for Me to work through the power of prayer. My angels are in constant combat to minister My words into the hearts of My people *(John 16:16).*

We had to wait until the time when My overcomers would come out of man's ideas of being religious and would allow Me to live My life in them—to the point where they allow Me to be in control and be the head of My people. Now, we can work together as a joint venture between Heaven and Earth. I had to wait for the emergence of My Branch. The woman had to bring forth the man-child. My body had to bring forth the Branch *(Isaiah 11:1-5; Ezekiel 10:1-18; Revelation 12).*

The church is now in pain; she is now travailing to bring forth My man-child. But this is only a part of what is happening. At the same time there is a great war going on in Heaven. Things happen first in the Spiritual Realm, before My people see the events acted out upon Earth. Satan, in his kingdom, has seven heads with seven crowns also *(Isaiah 66:8; Revelation 12:3).*

Satan has drawn one-third of the angels of Heaven, and they are about to be cast down upon the Earth. He is doing everything he can to stop My church, My body from bringing forth the man-child, but to no avail. My Branch, My man-child, is coming forth to rule the nations in My Kingdom with a rod of iron *(Revelation 12: 4).*

After the man-child is delivered, Satan will know that he is about to be cast upon the Earth. Satan will persecute the church, or the mother of My man-child. But the mother will be taken into the wilderness upon wings supplied by My anointed ones. There, My body will find rest. Satan's anger will rise up against others of My body, but will not prevail *(Revelation 12: 12, 13).*

My sons, encourage My people with the anointing that I have placed upon you. You are the ones anointed to boldly stand up in the name of the Lord. Rise up, My sons! You will stand up and be My extended right hand, just as My power worked through you in bringing fire from Heaven and parting the sea. You will stand up and break the yoke of the anti-christ.

And it shall come to pass in that day that his burden shall be taken away from the shoulders of My people and his yoke off their necks. The neck shall be destroyed because of the anointing. Encourage My people, and tell them not to be afraid *(Isaiah 10:26-27, 63:12)*.

Stand up, My sons, you are My arms that I will use to chop off the terror, the powers of the high ones and leaders of world powers *(Isaiah 63:11, 10:26)*.

*   *   *

When My Branch comes forth, My Word and power will become flesh in My body, My corporate Christ. The people of My planting around the world will properly be called the International Branch of the Lion of Judah. My Spirit will be upon My people. These are My eyes sent forth over the Earth under the power of My seven spirits within My Holy Spirit: the spirit of wisdom, the spirit of understanding, the spirit of counsel, the spirit of power, the spirit of knowledge, the spirit of reverence for the Lord, and the spirit of judgment *(Isaiah 11:1-5)*.

When My people totally submit to Me, then I am able

to live My life in them and anoint them with these seven spirits of My Holy Spirit. This sevenfold spirit manifested in you, My sons, will bring down all problems that come before you. So that we, not by might nor by power, but by My Spirit, will go forth proclaiming that the Kingdom has come *(Isaiah 10:27, 11:1-5; Zechariah 46:7)*.

My sons, you have been obedient and by faith have acted to lay the foundation of My Kingdom through your obedience and understanding of what I have revealed— the little book that closes time and opens up eternity; the little book that tastes sweet but makes the belly bitter; the word that must be prophesied again before many peoples, nations, languages, and kings. All My people will know that I have sent you forth for this purpose *(Revelation 8:10)*.

My International Branch of the Lion of Judah will proclaim to the world: "WE COME IN THE NAME OF THE LORD OUR GOD. HE ALONE IS OUR RIGHTEOUSNESS." My Branch will cover the entire Earth giving fair judgments to the poor, and reclaiming the wealth and equity of the meek of the Earth. And I will speak through My Branch to slay the wicked with the breath of his lips and smite the Earth with the rod of his mouth. My glorious Branch is robed in righteousness and integrity *(Isaiah 11:1-5)*.

Then My name will be lifted up, and I will be known to all people. Jesus Christ will draw His people. All people will come to Me to be a part of My glory and rest. Then in that day, I will set My hand again the second time to gather the people out of the nations of the world. Exodus Number

Two will be even more glorious than our coming out of Egypt *(Isaiah 11; Jeremiah 23:5-9).*

I will also free My people from all of the bondages that have been placed upon them in the name of religion. All that seems righteous to the world religions may not be righteous in My sight. Woe to the pastors and church leaders that scatter My people, the sheep of My pasture. Let it be known that I will visit upon those church leaders the evil of their own doings *(Zechariah 13:7-9).*

Then I will gather the remnant of My people out of all the countries where I have driven them. I will again bring them together and will bless and prosper them. I will set up new leaders who will love and care for My people.

My people will learn to trust and won't fear, nor will they lack anything at all. Listen and understand, My sons, the days are now come that I will raise up My righteous Branch and I will appoint their king, and he will lead and prosper My people and will execute judgment and justice upon the Earth. In his day, I will unite Christianity and all its denominations with Islam and Judaism and its various groups into one glorious body—My International Branch *(Ezekiel 37:16-28).*

Understand this, My sons, we are going to do something so wonderful and spectacular that people will no longer celebrate the Passover by saying that the Lord lives with those who brought the children of Israel out of the land of Egypt. Rather, they will say the Lord lives with those who brought up and led the seed of the house of Israel out of the North Country and from all countries where I had driven them.

Then they shall dwell in their own land *(Jeremiah 23:5-8).*

My people dwelling in all nations of the world will be brought out of all countries and will become a mighty nation. Both Israel and Judah will be brought together upon the Holy Mountain of Israel, and there I will place My king over them all. Israel, as well as Judah, will no longer be two nations, nor will they be divided into two nations ever again *(Jeremiah 23:38).*

*   *   *

My people of Israel, having become believers in Me, and My people of Judah, whom the world calls Jews, are all of the same family of God. Can't both My family trees see that I have redeemed them? I have called each and every one by name. They are mine, and they belong to Me. When they pass through the deep waters, I will be with them and will even part the rivers of water as they pass through them. When they walk through the fire, they will not be burned; the flames won't even singe the hair on their heads *(Isaiah 43:1-2).*

I will say to the North, "Give up!" And to the South, "Keep not back!" Now is the time to bring My sons from far and My daughters from the very ends of the Earth. Let all people of all nations be gathered and brought together. Let them speak their piece, and let them hear the truth. Let all My people become a new nation, a one-world nation under the direction of God, the Father, through His Son, Jesus Christ, whose Spirit works in the hearts of His people.

I will rule through My body, My overcomers, My International Branch *(Isaiah 43:6)*.

You will look and see all those that I have gathered from afar—from the North and from the West and from all nations upon the Earth. All of those who have come to the land of Israel will be so many that the land will seem too small for all My people to dwell *(Zechariah 10:10, 11)*.

My sons, at this time, you will set up a standard to be established in every position of authority, both civil authority as well as priestly authority, in our royal priesthood. The plumbline or Branch standard will be raised before all people.

This standard of heavenly authority will draw My people from all countries. This will bring new meaning to My words. If I am lifted up from the Earth I will draw all men to Me. This standard will be for a sign to My people, and they will come and find rest and comfort in the glory of their land *(Zechariah 3:7-9, 4:9-10; Isaiah 11:10)*.

This word and truth will go to all corners of the Earth as it is spoken and broadcast from the capital, My Holy City, Jerusalem. This standard of Lord will flow over the entire Earth, and the Earth will be full of the knowledge of the Lord. All iniquity and evil will be removed from My land and My royal city, Jerusalem *(Revelation 11:3)*.

My Temple will be rebuilt upon My Holy Mountain. Did not I say to Zerubbabel that your hands have laid the foundation of this house, and have I not said that your hands shall finish it? The world may think that you have not acted upon My Word.

And don't you yourself think this as a small thing? My people from all over the Earth will see the plummet in your hand. The walls and the pillars will be established, and the people will see the plummet in your hand with those seven that I have chosen. They are the ones I have chosen to become eyes of the Lord. I will send them, and they will crisscross the entire Earth with My people as the army of God putting My Kingdom in order. These are My anointed ones, My two olive branches, walking in total submission to Me and My words spoken through them that set up My standard of the Lord over the whole Earth (*Zechariah 6:11-15, 4:10, 4:14; Revelation 11:1-14*).

I will give to you My two witnesses, and you shall prophesize to the world about the coming Kingdom over the networks of world communication for 1,260 days clothed in sackcloth. My two olive branches and the two candlesticks are what I will channel My power through. If anyone tries to hurt you or stand in your way, by speaking the words that I have put in your mouths, you will have fire come forth at your command and devour your enemies. If any man should hurt you in any way, that same person must be killed in the same way. You, My anointed ones, stand between Me and all the people upon the Earth (*Revelation 11:1-14*).

All the laws and powers of nature, I will place at your command, so that you may shut up the heavens so there is no rain in the days that you prophesize. You will be turning water into blood, and you will be able to strike the Earth with all types of plagues as often as I have you. Bringing

My people out of Egypt wasn't the main event. The seven trumpet judgments that are to come upon the Earth are our next performance.

*　*　*

Rise up, Moses and Elijah, My sons. My people must be told and taught the truth of who they are. Rise up, My sons. A new voice will be crying, not only in the wilderness, but My voice will be heard over the entire Earth. Inside all nations, the Word will ring loud and clear. My people, come forth. Come and enter into the Kingdom of your God. Prepare ye the way of the Lord *(Isaiah 41:1-4)*.

My people will respond and will learn the truth of who they are. And they will know that I, the Lord their God, has done this. They will see and understand their beginnings, and how their fathers turned from Me and how they were sent among the nations. But now, they will know that they are of the true and original seed of Abraham. You will see those who once despised Me are now ashamed and confounded. They will be as nothing in themselves. They will be totally empty, broken, and humbled.

Now they are able to be used as My army, My International Branch. Let them know that they have not been cast out; but I, their Lord, have chosen them as My Branch. Tell them not to fear. For I am now with them. Don't let them be discouraged. Come forth, My sons. I will strengthen you. I will help you. I will hold your right hand *(Isaiah 41:15, 16).*

The nations will see My righteous Branch come forth, and they will be afraid. They will see My Spirit revealed through My anointed Branch as they come together, helping and encouraging one another in perfect unity and equality *(Isaiah 41:5).*

As the poor and needy of My people seek food and water where there is none to be found, then I, the Lord, will hear them. I, the God of Israel, will open rivers in high places and will cause fountains to open up and will make pools of water in the wilderness, and springs of water will appear in dry desserts *(Isaiah 41:17-19).*

Listen to Me, Moses and Elijah. You are My servants whom I uphold, Mine elect in whom My soul delighteth. I have put My Spirit upon you. You will bring forth the judgment of the Lord, you will do this in righteousness, and you will speak tenderly to those that are bruised. Yes, you will judge all things in truth. Rest assured that you will not fail. And don't be discouraged until you have established this judgment upon the Earth *(Isaiah 42:1-7, 30:30-31).*

The nations of the world are waiting, and through you I will give a new breath of life to My people. They will be lifted up with a new spirit of excitement. My Branch will open blind eyes and bring out the prisoners from the prisons. I'm telling you these things before they happen. All things will be changed. The old will pass away, and all things will become new *(Isaiah 42:7).*

Tell My people to sing a new song, and praise the Lord their God for what He is going to do. Let all My people over the entire Earth praise the Lord and give Him glory. For I, the Lord, will go before them as a mighty man stirring up jealousy that will cause war to come upon our enemies. My sons, I have been long and patient. I have been still, I have refrained Myself, but now I must come forth mightily to destroy and devour. The mountains will be wasted and the rivers will be dried up *(Revelation 15:3; Isaiah 12:2, 42:10, 41:4).*

Yet through this, I will bring My people, the blind, by a way that they did not know about. I will lead them in paths they did not know, and the darkness will become light before them. The rough and the crooked places will be made straight. This is what I am going to do for My people.

I will never forsake them. My people who have been far from Me, when they see this, will be greatly ashamed of all their self-centered pride and will repent from worshipping their idols of self-interests. My people are deaf, and they are blind, but they must see and hear the truth *(Isaiah 41:16).*

*   *   *

My sons, you have the general time frames as to the opening of the book of seals. The book was opened, and the first seal was broken on April 10, 1984, which released My body to come into unity as My man on a white horse. On October 10, 1984, the second seal was broken, and this allowed the forces of evil to take peace from the Earth. On April 10, 1985, the third seal was broken to allow the fall of mysterious Babylon so that the wealth of the unrighteous can be transferred into My Kingdom.

The fourth seal was broken on October 10, 1985, allowing famines, pestilence, and attacks of beasts of the field on people. The fifth seal was broken on April 10, 1986, allowing the world to persecute My body, and many of My people will be slain for their testimony. On October 10, 1986, the sixth seal was broken to allow for the physical signs in the heavens and great earthquakes to take place upon the Earth *(Revelation 6:1-15)*.

On April 10, 1987, as I broke the seventh seal, a period of silence began in Heaven for a half hour. This is not a half hour on Earth, but a half hour in Heaven where the measure of time is one day in Heaven equals 1,000 years on the Earth. So a short time of only a half hour in Heaven is what many on Earth consider a long time. The one-half hour in Heaven is the same as 20 years and 83 days upon the Earth. I explained this to My people in the Bible. So the prophetic timetable of Earth time was extended, rather than shortened, while we are in our half hour of silence in Heaven. Even though the prophetic clock stopped, the seals have already been released for good and evil *(Revelation 81-6)*.

You see, My sons, I am allowing My BRANCH the time to fulfill all My prophetic words that I have spoken to My people. This is the time to prepare My people for the tasks that I have set before them. My sons, you must teach My people what I have revealed to you. You must speak this truth to My people. Teach and train My people for war in the spiritual world. My army of God must be formed around the truth that I have revealed to you. This will involve sending you to many parts of the world and your speaking these truths.

My people over the whole Earth must hear My everlasting gospel and the Kingdom-come message will be delivered to every nation, kindred, and tongue. No one will have an excuse. Everyone will have heard you describe the next main event that will be even more spectacular than our Exodus out of Egypt. The second Exodus will be our Exodus out of all worldly governments by way of our seven trumpet judgments *(Jeremiah 23:5-9)*.

These trumpet judgments will fulfill many prophecies of My prophets of old. This single event will bring Israel and Judah together. It will cause the fall of Babylon. It will be the destruction of Gog and Magog, and it will be culminated by My return to Earth with all My saints. During this time, you will see the full mystery of Babylon revealed as it pertains to the seven financial mountains, the restoration of the ancient city and its destruction. This will be done by the stone cut out of the mountain without hands, My Kingdom overtaking Satan's anti-christ kingdom even before it is established *(Daniel 2:44)*.

Some of My people, being led by My Spirit, are working by faith without a full understanding. They are building properties that will be used for havens of rest in the wilderness and in the mountains. These havens will be established in the nations of the world. These properties will be provided for My people when Satan is cast upon the Earth. This is for the woman who flees into the wilderness because of the dragon's anger when he realizes My man-child, My Branch, has been birthed into overcomers. These will be places of the Second Passover.

Just as My people came out of Egypt with great wealth, people coming out of the north countries will come with great glory in the form of the silver and gold of their captors. "Did I not say the silver and the gold are mine?" sayeth the Lord. I will protect My people and the glory in these places of refuge by a cloud of smoke by day and the shining of a flaming fire by night *(Zechariah 2:8)*.

* * *

My sons, the four angels that I placed on the four corners of the Earth on June 13, 1984, are still holding and restraining the forces of evil. The four winds will blow destruction from the seven trumpet judgments. They will remain there until My special forces, My overcomers, My man-child, and My Branch are completely sealed. My candlesticks and My two olive branches will clean up any unfinished work during the time of the sounding of trumpets *(Revelation 7:1-4, 11:4; Ezekiel 9:1-4)*.

These overcomers, the four beasts in Ezekiel's vision, are going wherever the head looks. I will direct them to all corners of the Earth, having four wheels full of eyes and letting Me direct them through the wheel within the wheel. This is the principle of seven eyes upon one stone or plummet standard. My sons, you are men dressed in linen on the inside and men dressed in sackcloth on the outside; but as you speak to My people, they will see and be stirred. You will see many that first appeared meek and lowly rise to the occasion and become heroes in My spiritual army. You will see that the cream surely does rise to the top. My angels will marvel at the wheel, saying, "O wheel!" *(Ezekiel 101:18)*.

My overcomers will bring in multitudes so great that they won't be able to be numbered. They will be stones placed within My Temple of all My people, each being a perfect stone in proper position of My living Temple. My prayer warriors upon the Earth have filled the golden vials full of odors, which are the prayers of the saints. These vials were poured upon My golden altar on April 10, 1985, the day I broke the seventh seal and the beginning of the one-half hour of silence in Heaven. The smoke of incense, the sweet aroma of prayer ascended up before My Father *(Revelation 5:8, 8:1-4)*.

Soon, My sons, the censers will be full, filled with fire, and will be handed to you to be cast upon the Earth as My Word and work of judgment *(Ezekiel 10:2)*.

The seven angels with the seven trumpets are waiting for the word to act. But prior to this, My sons, judgment must come upon My church. For it is written that judgment begins at the House of God. Judgment must pass through My people. All My people who yearn for righteousness have been noted, and all those covered by the blood of My Son are secure. But all those who have not accepted the free gift of My Son will be judged, and all My carnally minded will pass through judgment. I will no longer allow My house to be defiled. My body, My bride, must now be spotless *(Revelation 8:6; Isaiah 51:4-6)*.

My people will all be judged. And the streets will flow with the blood of the slain. The churches, as well as the whole land, will be full of blood. I shall not spare nor have pity anymore. This is the day that I must judge My people *(Ezekiel 9:1-11)*.

Near the end of the half hour of silence in Heaven, there will be unity in much of My body—the ones making up My army of overcomers. By the summer of 2007, My International Branch of the Lion of Judah will have fulfilled the great commission. No one alive upon the Earth will have any excuse. No one will be able to say he does not understand My free gift of salvation by the blood of the Lamb of God.

My people will all know the perimeters of the Christ-controlled life and the joys of Kingdom living. The wealth of the world will have flown from the unrighteous of the world to the people of My Kingdom. Then the entire universe will be waiting for the Earth to be cleansed in preparation of the 1,000-year kingdom of My Son upon Earth. By then, all people upon the Earth will have been shaken by great earthquakes, and they will hear voices from Heaven with lightning and thunder.

The entire world will know that My seven angels with the seven trumpets are about ready to sound *(Revelation 8:5)*.

Even after all this, the leaders of the northern nations refuse to let My people go. Their hearts have been hardened. But even Gog will thrust My people out of his country, just as the pharaohs did out of Egypt. And Gog's armies will be destroyed near Lebanon upon the mountains of Israel. This will be the same judgment that the pharaoh received. All the armies of Magog and the armies of all the nations led by Gog will be destroyed.

My son, the second act of freeing My people will proceed. Moses, at your spoken word, at your spoken command, we will begin the steps to free My people from bondage.

* * *

As the *first angel sounds his trumpet,* hail and fire mingled with blood—the blood of all living creatures, including people in the sky, covering the one-third of the Earth that we judge—will be cast down to the Earth. One-third of all green grass and green trees will burn with thick smoke covering the ground *(Revelation 8:7).*

Then, My son, Moses, a few weeks later you will speak the command for the *second trumpet* to be sounded. It will appear as if a great mountain has been cast into the sea with such a great explosion that the waves will roar. The northern and eastern parts of the sea around Russia and China will be turned into blood, and the sea will burn as a great fire. All ships and submarines, as well as every form of life within this area of the sea, will be destroyed. One-third of the entire sea will be turned into blood. My son, you will see that the weapons created for war against My people are used to cleanse the Earth through judgment by the Lord. And you will see more of this as you order the other trumpets to be blown.

As you order the *third trumpet* to sound, you will see how the star wars technology will be used for My purpose. And I also want to remind you, My son, of what the word "wormwood" means in the Russian language. Remember the word "Chernobyl," the Russian nuclear explosion? The atomic contamination that polluted the water? Now, My son, you can see that the great star that falls from Heaven, burning as a lamp that turns one-third of all the rivers and fountains of waters upon Earth bitter. Many people upon the Earth will die as a result of these bitter waters.

When you order the *fourth trumpet* to sound, the world will realize they have an environmental problem. Smoke will be pouring from the one-third part of the Earth burned and from the one-third of the seal. The air will be contaminated. The atmosphere will be so filled with smoke that only one-third of the brightness of the sun will appear through the smoke. The sun and moon will only be one-third as bright. And one-third of the stars will not be seen at all.

After this, Moses and Elijah, My two witnesses upon the Earth, will prophesize 1,260 days. They will appear on worldwide TV dressed in sackcloth. The satellite will circle the Earth 22,000 miles out in space. This is the angel, John, who flies through the midst of Heaven saying with a loud voice, "Woe, woe, woe to the inhabitants of the Earth. Even worse judgments are about to fall upon the Earth when the next three angels sound their trumpets" *(Revelation 11:3, 14:6)*.

Moses and Elijah, you both will prophesize for 42 months as My two witnesses speaking to My people. During this time, many upon the Earth will try to slay you; but you will be protected and empowered through My anointing. During this time, I will put myself, the God of Heaven and Earth, at your command.

If anyone tries to hurt you as you speak, I will devour your enemies. I have given you the power that you will use to close up Heaven so that no rain will fall upon the Earth during the days of your prophecy. And you have power to turn water into blood and smite the Earth with plagues just as we did in the Old Testament times *(Revelation 11:4-6)*.

During this time many upon the Earth will seek death; but death won't be found as a way of escape.

* * *

When the *fifth angel's trumpet sounds*, a star will fall from Heaven and will open the bottomless pit. This will release the smoke of a great furnace, and out of the smoke will come locusts upon the Earth. These locusts will look like horses prepared for battle, having faces of men with gold crowns on their heads. Their hair will be long, and their teeth will be as sharp as lion's teeth; their breasts plates will be of iron, they will roar like jets and will sting with their tails. Their power to torment all mankind who refuse the free gift of salvation will last for five months. The first woe is passed.

The king over these locusts, the angel of the bottomless

pit, named "Abaddon" in Hebrew, will make war against you, My two anointed ones. He will be allowed, after the sixth trumpet judgment, to overcome you and will kill both of you. Your dead bodies will lie in the streets of Jerusalem for three days *(Revelation 9:11)*.

These will be three days of ecstatic celebration on Earth. They will think that they have finally defeated the power of God. This will be reminiscent of the celebration Satan had when he saw Me die on the cross. After three days, Satan and his cronies will again be struck with terror, this time by seeing you, My two anointed ones, resurrected by My Father to life by sending you back to Earth to reclaim your bodies *(Revelation 11:7-14)*.

Then, when you have stepped back into your bodies, I will speak from Heaven so that the whole Earth will hear Me say, "Come up hither!" And you both will ascend just as I did from the Mount of Olives in clouds of glory as our enemies watch in shock. Then, within the hour, I will shake Jerusalem with a great earthquake that will destroy one-tenth of the city. This earthquake will kill 7,000 people, but then many will turn to Me even then. They will be saved, giving the glory to Me. Now, the second woe is passed. The third and final one will come quickly.

Gog will take this opportunity, after you two have been raised to Heaven, to bring all of his armies together in a final effort to defeat the powers of My Father by destroying My people, whom we released and brought back to the land of Israel after the fifth trumpet sounded. He expects to take a great spoil of the wealth brought from all countries by My people, Israel, returning to be one again with Judah. My sons, when the sixth angel sounds, you will order the sixth angel to loose the four angels, which are bound in the great river Euphrates. These angels are prepared for this year, this month, this day, and this very hour to slay one-third of the men *(Revelation 9:13-21)*.

The armies of Russia, Germany, Libya, Ethiopia, Iran, and Turkey will come together with a force of 200 million soldiers equipped with modern, motorized weapons, but appearing to John as horses. One-third of mankind will be killed by fire, smoke, and brimstone from modern weapons *(Ezekiel 38, 39; Revelation 9:16-18)*.

Gog, the leader of all these nations, will be the one who raises himself to power by defeating Egypt and taking advantage of America's failures in Kosovo. This man, Gog, is none other than Saddam Heussein of Iraq, the king of Babylon. As My people returned and began rebuilding Jerusalem after the fifth trumpet sounded, Satan, at the same time, centered his power in the ancient city of Babylon that Saddam started rebuilding in the 1960's.

This same man, now known as Gog, will lead this invasion, gathering all of his forces within only a few miles of Jerusalem and will shake his fist at My Holy Mountain. My fury will then rise up, and I will cause a great earthquake in the land of Israel. And I will cause every man's weapon to be turned against his brother. There will be mass confusion and panic until they totally destroy themselves *(Isaiah 10:34, Jeremiah 23: 9).*

The armies shall fall with Lebanon on the mountains of Israel. After I have regathered the whole house of Israel out of their enemy's hands, then shall they know Me as THE LORD, OUR RIGHTEOUSNESS, who delivered His people out of the North Country.

* * *

As the *seventh trumpet sounds*, it will be the last trumpet of God and many on Earth will be in rapture. But the Father has chosen to leave many overcomers on the Earth and the thunders are their encouragement.

Even after this, many people will not repent and turn from worshipping devils and idols of gold. They will continue to murder, steal, and practice perverted sex acts. Satan still has them under control by the deception of drugs *(Revelation 11:15-19).*

Then, My son, I will send another mighty angel from My throne to the Earth with our little book. This will be the knowledge of Kingdom living. My angel will speak seven messages to My people on Earth *(Revelation 10:2-11).*

Many people will not understand, but those that I want to understand will understand what I want each one to understand. The seven thunders are the seven promises to My overcomers. When the seventh angel sounds his trumpet, there will be the great voice of many voices. All the hosts of Heaven will be speaking together as one voice: THE KINGDOMS OF THIS WORLD ARE

BECOME THE KINGDOMS OF OUR LORD AND OF
HIS CHRIST, AND HE SHALL REIGN FOREVER AND
EVER *(Revelation 11:15).*

Then the great thunders sound.

The First Thunder Sounds: To him that overcometh, will
I give to eat of the tree of life, which is in the midst of the
paradise of God *(Revelation 2:7).*

The Second Thunder Sounds: He that overcometh shall
not be hurt of the second death *(Revelation 2:11).*

The Third Thunder Sounds: To him that overcometh, will
I give to eat of the hidden manna and will give him a white
stone, and in the stone a new name written, which no man
knoweth except he that receiveth it *(Revelation 2:17).*

The Fourth Thunder Sounds: And he that overcometh
and keepeth My works unto the end, to him will I give power
over the nations. And he shall rule them with a rod of iron as
the vessels of a potter shall they be broken to shivers, even as
I received of My Father *(Revelation 2:26, 27).*

The Fifth Thunder Sounds: He that overcometh the same
shall be clothed in white raiment, and I will not blot out
his name from the book of life; but I will confess his name
before My Father and before His angels *(Revelation 3:5).*

The Sixth Thunder Sounds: He that overcometh, will I
make a pillar in the Temple of My God, and he shall go no
more out. I will write upon him the name of My God and
the name of the city of My God, New Jerusalem, which
cometh down out of Heaven from My God and I will write
upon him My new name *(Revelation 3:12).*

The Seventh Thunder Sounds: To him that overcometh,

will I grant to sit with Me in My throne, even as I also overcame and sat down with My Father in His throne. Then the heavenly hosts will break out singing and worshipping the Lord and saying, "We give thee thanks, O God Almighty, because thou hast taken to thee thy great power and hast reigned" *(Revelation 3:21).*

*   *   *

And after these things there will be a great voice again of many people in Heaven saying, "Alleluia, salvation, glory, honor, and power unto the Lord our God. For true and righteous are His judgments; for He has judged the great whore, which did corrupt the Earth with her fornication and hath avenged the blood of His servants at her hand" *(Revelation 19:1, 2).*

My sons, I have revealed much to you. The great whore controls My people of all nations, and all the kings of the Earth have committed fornication and have become drunk with the wine of her adultery.

Over Mystery Babylon sits Spiritual Babylon.

In the Spiritual Realm, Babylon, the woman arrayed in purple and scarlet, decked with gold, precious stones, and pearls; and having a golden cup in her hand, full of abominations, controls the physical.

Mystery Babylon controls the powers of the world by controlling the finances of the world. There is a small number of individuals from less than a dozen families who control the seven mountains that the woman sits upon.

The seven mountains are the seven central banks of the world that control everything else *(Revelation 17:1-18)*.

The cause and effect of every aspect of life on Earth are directed by the supply of finances. The powers of every kingdom are moved by the powers of finance to travel the road desired. Over this central power sits Satan as the invisible president and chairman of the board of directors.

Satan is the beast that controls Mystery Babylon, and he is striving to put his house in order by setting up his king, the anti-christ, as the head of Babylon. His goal is to have Babylon the world center for his king and false prophet, and to put down the Kingdom of God on Earth.

But, My sons, we will meet Satan and fight, and My people will overcome and set up the Kingdom of God. My Branch has been planted, and it will grow into My man-child that overcomes *(Revelation 12:1-12)*.

Everything is in perfect order as the Father has directed, and everything has its time. Now is the time to bring forth the Kingdom of God. Everything written about the anti-christ standing as the abomination of desolation is for a time, but not of this generation and time. We are going to have our rest. We are going to have the kingdom on Earth for one day, our 1,000-year day, and then Satan will again be allowed to bring forth his anti-christ. He will not be successful even then. We will defeat him again with the seven bowl judgments upon the Earth. Then will be the day of anti-christ and Armageddon and the rapture of all saints upon the Earth—all to the glory of God.

BOUNDARIES TO ENTERING THE KINGDOM OF GOD

The Holy Bible is God's blueprint to build a world of righteousness as well as the blueprint for each individual to become righteous. His plan is to prepare each person to be a building block within the Kingdom of God. In our present world, each individual has tremendous opposition from the world and the principalities and the powers of Satan's kingdom that battle inside the minds of all individuals upon the Earth.

We, as individuals, are already defeated in our own strength. But through taking upon ourselves the full armor of God in total submission to the Lord Jesus Christ, we are no longer defeated but victorious in leading the Christ-controlled life. The boundaries for living within the Kingdom of God are in Christ Jesus. Any thought or action outside the life of Jesus Christ is outside the boundaries of the Kingdom of God.

Any self-directed thought, followed by a self-directed action, is outside the boundaries of Kingdom living and is destructive not only to the individual, but also destructive to the body of Christ and the Kingdom of God. On the other hand, every Christ-controlled thought and directed thought followed by an action are constructive and contributes to the body of Christ and the Kingdom of God.

The key to living within the boundaries of the Kingdom

of God is keeping the mind upon Christ as an attitude of living your life in and for Jesus Christ. This is done by no longer exercising your own will in choosing anything or making any decisions outside the will of Christ Jesus. This is more than an attitude and this is more than submission and this is more than faith. Although it involves attitude, submission, and faith, it is letting and knowing that Christ is living in your body—not only in your body, but in your life as well. This is submitting to power, submitting to peace, and submitting to joy in place of fear, in place of frustration, and in place of worry. This is the knowing that you *know*. It is knowing that it is no longer you who thinks with this mind, but it is the mind of Christ that is operating through His Spirit in your spirit.

The Spirit of the Lord is allowed total control—giving you the Lord's wisdom, the Lord's understanding, the Lord's counsel, the Lord's authority, the Lord's knowledge, the Lord's quick understanding, and the Lord's judgment. Every thought must be given to the Lord to perform the will of the Lord in every action. We must let the Lord do good to them who hate us through our own physical bodies, giving blessings and a spirit of love when we are cursed with an attitude. Every possession and everything you love are no longer under your control. Every relationship is letting Christ, by His Spirit living in you, exercise His life through you. The Christ in you is your only basis for any relationship. This is not a one-to-one basis only, but a relationship anchored in Christ Jesus where you allow the Lord to have His will and expression.

The boundaries for living within the Kingdom of God are:

Be born again. Thou shalt worship the Lord thy God and serve Him only. Thou shalt not tempt the Lord thy God. Preach the Kingdom of God. Call sinners to repentance. Love your enemies. Do good to those who hate you. Bless those who curse you. Pray for them who despitefully use you. Turn the other cheek. Do not resist, even when stolen from. Give to anyone who asks. Don't ask for anything in return. Do to others as you want them to do unto you. Love your enemies. Do good and lend, hoping for nothing. Be merciful. Judge not others. Condemn not others. Forgive others. Deny yourself and follow the Lord. Give your life to the Lord. Witness for Christ. Confess Christ before men. Receive others. Don't deny children. Heal the sick. Cast out demons. Pray the Lord's prayer. Take no thought to your life. Don't worry. Seek the Kingdom of God. Sell what you have to give to those in need. Be of strong mind. Determine to let your light shine. Be always ready to meet Christ. Strive to enter the straight gate to God's Kingdom. Humble yourselves before men. Take the lowest position. Forsake all that you have for the Lord. Pray and don't faint. Give what is Caesar's to Caesar. Give what is God's to God. Pray that ye enter not into temptation. Wait upon the Lord for His power to come forth in you. Go in meekness. Hunger and thirst after righteousness. Be of pure heart. Search the scriptures for truth. Judge not according to appearances. Serve and forgive one another. Submit to God's designated authority. Love one another as Jesus loves you. Let the Lord's joy be fulfilled in you. Be sanctified through the word of truth. Seek to be one in Christ. Repent and be baptized. Receive the gift of the Holy Spirit. Obey God rather than men. Rejoice that you are counted worthy to suffer shame for Christ. Be not a respecter of persons, one above another. Reckon yourselves to be dead to sin. Let the strong bear the infirmities of the weak, not to please ourselves. Let no man seek his own, but every man another's welfare. Follow after love. Live and walk in the power of the Holy Spirit. Endeavor to keep unity of the Spirit of Christ. Be renewed in the spirit of your mind. Put on the new man of righteousness and holiness. Don't be angry. Let no corrupt communication proceed from your mouth. Speak that which is good and edifying. Grieve not the Holy Spirit. Seek the will of God. Be constantly filled with the Holy Spirit. Give thanks, always, for all things. Put on the whole armor of God. Esteem others better than yourself. Take on the mind of Christ. Do all things without murmuring or disputing. Forget things past; press toward the high calling of God. Let no man judge you, only the Lord. Set your affections on things above. Let the peace of God rule in your heart. Let the Word of God dwell in you. Do all things in the name of Jesus, and give thanks to God. Let your speech be with grace. Know how to answer every man. Rejoice evermore. Quench not the spirit. Despise not prophesying. Prove all things. Hold fast to that which is good. Abstain from the appearance of evil. Neglect not the gift that is in you. Live righteously and Godly in this present world. Be zealous to do good works. Show meekness to all men. Be careful to maintain good works. Despise not the *chastening of the Lord. Faint not when rebuked by the Lord. Lift up the hands that hang down and the feeble knees. Be not forgetful to entertain strangers; some have entertained angels. Remember those who are in bonds. Remember those who suffer adversity as being yourself. Let your conversation be without covetousness. Be content with such things as you have. Be not carried away with strange doctrines. Offer the sacrifice of praise to God continually. Be perfect in every good work to do His will. Let patience have her perfect work. Let every man be swift to hear, slow to speak, and slow to wrath. Be doers of the Word and not listeners only. Visit the fatherless and widows in their affliction. Keep yourselves unspotted from the world. Submit yourselves to God, and resist the devil. Rejoice not in boasting; all such rejoicing is evil. If you know to do good and don't do it, it is sin. Be patient as to the coming of the Lord. Grudge not one against another. Swear not; let your ye be ye and your nay be nay. Confess your faults one to another. Abstain from fleshly lusts, which war against the soul. Put to silence the ignorance of men with well doing. Love the brotherhood. Fear God. Honor the King. Endure grief, suffering wrongfully, for conscience toward God. Wives, be subject to your husbands. Husbands, honor your wives as the weaker vessel. Be of one mind. Cast your cares upon the Lord. Add to your faith, virtue, and to virtue, knowledge. Add to your temperance, patience. Add to your godliness, kindness and love. Love not the world nor the things that are in the world. Love not in words but deeds. Keep yourselves from idols. Some save with compassion. Some save with fear, pulling them out of the fire. Receive not the mark of the beast. Thou shalt have no other gods. Thou shalt not make any graven images to worship. Thou shalt not take the Lord's name in vain. Remember the Sabbath day to keep it holy. Honor thy father and thy mother. Thou shalt not kill. Thou shalt not commit adultery. Thou shalt not steal. Thou shalt not bear false witness. Thou shalt not covet thy neighbor's possessions. Honor Me.*

Before the Flood

From the time of creation to the time of Abraham, memory has been hidden from all generations. Archeological discoveries of this period have been few, and the understanding that the world believes is at best a speculation. However, the world has been taught to believe in someone's opinion that had a motive or agenda.

I will now present my story of how I think it was before the flood, based on scripture and other ancient writings. Common sense and a few clues are the main basis for this argument.

Based on the dates revealed by calculating mathematically the interior passage of the pyramid, the Exodus out of Egypt is believed to have begun in 1453 BC. This was about 1,950 years after the flood, which happened about 2400 BC. According to the ancient manuscripts *Adam and Eve*, Enoch was 20 years old when Seth, Adam's son, died. Enoch's son, Methuselah, lived 969 years and died just prior to the flood.

Based on the timetable of Seth's life, we can determine that Seth was born 23 years after Adam and Eve left the garden and after seven years of grieving over Abel's death. According to this manuscript, Able was about 15 years old when he was slain by Cain.

Cain had a twin sister, Luluwa. Abel also had a twin sister. Adam and Eve desired to have Cain marry Abel's sister, and they desired for Abel to marry Cain's sister.

After the burial of Abel, Adam and Eve grieved for 140 days. Then when Cain was 17 years old, he took his sister, Luluwa, into marriage without his parents' consent. He took her away from the mountain where Adam and Eve lived in a cave called the *cave of treasures*.

From this point, Adam told his other children and grandchildren not to associate with any of Cain's children.

The date of creation and leaving the Garden of Eden was about 4931 BC.

Adam lived 930 years, and the average life span appears to have been about 900 years—until the second generation after the flood. Noah was 600 years old at the time of the flood and lived to be 950 years old.

The population started, evidently, with many multiple births: with brothers marrying sisters while in their teens.

With extended life spans, the period of child-bearing for each couple would have been for 500 years or more. So one couple could conceivably have had 500 children during their life span.

A person living 900 years would have learned a tremendous amount of knowledge about the Earth and the heavens as well as creative thinking to invent mathematics and other things. They would have known all the minerals and known how to develop metal and glass. When the Earth was filled with these aged wise men of knowledge, they must have all been creative geniuses.

With the births being very regular and frequent and the deaths being very, very rare, the population would have grown tremendously fast. In the 1,754 years from creation to the flood, it must have been years of tremendous development and invention, probably way beyond what we see upon the Earth today. And the population of the world was most likely greater than today.

This technology could have been above ours without the same source of energy that we see upon the Earth today. The Earth was different before the flood. The Earth evidently had a different axis with the effect of having the same weather year-round. There may have been an ice shield around the Earth with the dew or moisture falling at night without rain.

So before the flood, the world was full of billions of geniuses who had no language barriers. Then, all at once, a catastrophe happens: it rains 40 days and 40 nights, springing up on the Earth unexpectedly. Water destroys everything. There are no archeological remains of pre-flood life because all the evidence is probably at the deepest point in the oceans. The entire Earth was probably washed right down to bedrock, with the exception of the lowlands.

The flood was a starting over point for planet Earth. Within a year, I'm sure it looked like a fresh garden springing up.

The world before the flood evidently became materialistic, and the people turned completely away from following the Lord.

In this materialistic world, Noah was hated and ridiculed by the people. Noah was probably a loner that did not use all the technology available to the rest of the world.

In that day, it was probably like someone trying to build a rocket ship and launching pad from his garage. Noah built a boat in his backyard when no one had ever seen it rain. It seems like the Lord chooses what the world calls *weak* people to do great things. Noah was that one man who was able to hear God's voice, and he was obediently following a mission given to him by the Lord to build an Ark that took 100 years to build.

The book *Adam and Eve* states that the Lord told Adam there would be a flood, and Adam told his son to place his body inside the Ark. On Adam's deathbed he spoke to his son, Seth, as recorded in the second book of *Adam and Eve.*

2 Adam and Eve 8:9-13

9. *O Seth , my son, the moment I am dead take ye my body and wind it up with myrah, aloes, and cassia, and leave me here in this cave of treasures in which are all these tokens which God gave us from the garden.*

10. *O, my son, hereafter shall a flood come and overwhelm all creatures and leave only eight souls.*

11. *But, O my Son, let those whom it will leave out from among your children at that time, take my body with them out of this cave; and when they have taken it with them, let the eldest among them command his children to lay my body in a ship until the flood and they come out of the ship.*

12. *Then they shall take my body and lay it in the middle of the Earth, shortly after they have been saved from the waters of the flood.*

13. *For the place where my body shall be laid is the middle of the Earth; God shall come from thence and shall save all our kindred.*

Adam had lived 930 years. About 400 years later, according to the ancient manuscript *The Secrets of Enoch*, Enoch was taken to Heaven for 60 days and returned with the 366 books he had written. He gave his sons instructions as recorded in *The Secrets of Enoch*.

Secrets of Enoch 47:1, 2

1. *And now, my children, lay thought on your hearts, mark well the words of your father, which are all come to you from the Lord's lips.*

2. *Take these books of your father's handwriting and read them. For the books are many and in them you will learn all the Lord's works, all that has been from the beginning of creation, and will be till the end of time.*

Secrets of Enoch 48:6

6. *Thus I make known to you, my children, and distribute the books to your children, into all your generations, and amongst the nations who shall have this sense to fear God, let them require them, and may they come to love them more than any food or earthly sweets, and read them and apply themselves to them.*

The Bible outlines Enoch's life.

Genesis 5:21-23

21. *Enoch lived sixty and five years, and begat Methuselah.*

22. *Enoch walked with God after he begat Methuselah three hundred years and begat sons and daughters.*

23. *And Enoch walked with God: and he was not; for God took him.*

Noah was Enoch's great grandson and was born many years before Enoch was translated into Heaven. Noah entered the Ark about five hundred years later when he was 600 years old.

The Secrets of Enoch say that Enoch was taken to Heaven on the exact day and hour of his birth 365 years later.

Adam leaves instructions for his body to be taken to the middle of the Earth after the flood.

The monument most perfectly located in the center of the Earth is the pyramid of Giza. The measurements of the base are 365 sacred cubits on each side. The secrets so far revealed in the pyramid are beyond the knowledge known to men. The pyramid seems to have Enoch's signature written all over it.

Near the great pyramid is the Sphinx—the lion with the oversized man's head. Underneath the Sphinx is an unopened chamber as well as a smaller chamber under the Sphinx's right paw. The modern day seer, Edgar Cace, stated that the hall of records would be found under the right paw of the Sphinx.

It appears that the knowledge of Enoch could very well be tied to the great pyramid. And it would seem that Noah and the animals of the ark might be symbolized in the Sphinx. The original face of the man on the Sphinx may have actually been Adam's face.

The Ark landed on Mount Ararat in the northern section of Turkey. After it landed and the animals were released, the eight people probably lived in the Ark for a considerable time. They probably used it to transport themselves to another location. They may have disassembled it and used the material for other structures. It is natural that anyone would recycle everything to get a new start.

I suspect that Noah explored much of the Earth during his remaining 300 years on Earth. I also suspect that Noah was in Egypt, the actual center of the landmass of the world. Noah's expertise was in boat building, and at that time he was the best in the world.

The earliest known civilization is recorded on the island of Crete. They had multi-story buildings, elegant art and paintings; and they were expert boatsmen. My guess is that Noah himself chose to live there, and the future generations born into his family became great boat builders and sailors; and they established trade all over the world.

Archeologists say that the ruler of Minoa had the presage of an Egyptian pharaoh, and the name *Minoa* actually referred to an individual or ruler. It doesn't take a lot of imagination to get *Noah* out of *Minoa*.

It would seem that Noah settled on Crete, and his four sons and their wives settled in the four directions of the compass. It would seem that Shem settled in Egypt and completed the assigned mission given by Adam to place his body in the middle of the Earth.

If Noah and his late children were great sea-faring people, these ships going throughout the world could explain the mysteries of the lost cultures, such as the Mayan civilization of South America.

One of the sons of Noah, Ham, had a son named Cush,

and one of Cush's sons was named Nimrod. Nimrod became a mighty hunter and established the kingdom of Babel. The kingdom later came to be called Babylon after the languages were given to divide the people and the Tower of Babel was destroyed.

It appears that the nations in the Middle East came from Ham. The northern nations, including Eastern Europe and Russia, came from Japeth.

Shem's name means *hearing one*. He lived 600 years and had many children. Abraham, the father of all the tribes of Israel, was born in the lineage of Shem seven generations after the flood—about 350 years later.

THE GREAT PYRAMID

The Great Pyramid of Giza is easily the most massive building ever known to have been erected on Earth. There is no building more accurately aligned to the true cardinal points on the compass. The pyramid stones, weighing up to 70 tons each, are finely joined to a degree of 1/50 of an inch—roughly the thickness of one hair on your head. The base of the building covers 21 acres of land.

Nobody alive today knows for certain how the pyramid was erected, how long it took to build, or how its near perfect alignments were achieved. It is truly a work of art.

It is aligned with the Earth's four cardinal points and at the exact center of the geometrical quadrant formed by the Nile Delta. It is located at the exact center of the Earth's land surface—the geographical center of the whole land mass, including the Americas and Antarctica.

The messianic triangle began with the birth of Christ in 2 BC. His crucifixion in 33 AD opened the grand gallery or the way, the truth, and the life to all people.

The basic unit of measurement is exactly one-ten-millionth of the Earth's mean polar radius. The pyramid's designed square base has a side measuring 365.242 of the same units, a figure identical to the number of days in a solar year.

Other figures give the Earth's orbital distance around the sun, the distance from the Earth to the sun, and a cyclical period of over 25,000 years.

The Great Pyramid seems to be an architectural symbol for planet Earth. The pyramid's geometry combines all the data into an elegant identification of planet Earth and expresses meaning in how they relate to each other in foretelling past, present, and future events.

It appears that the pyramid was built in 2623 BC and was symbolized by the beginning entry into the pyramid. It is thought by most Bible scholars that the flood occurred about 2400 BC. So people whose knowledge was beyond what technology shows us today probably built the pyramid before the flood. People in that time period lived approximately ten times longer than the average life span of people today, and they were able to expand their learning by the same extended period.

It appears that the pyramid is a monument or witness carefully planned and premeditated for some future generations after a great deluge or world catastrophe.

A fragment of early literature came to light through certain manuscripts found in Russia and Servia, preserved only in the Slavonic language. Within these writings of *The Secrets of Enoch* are an overview of creation and a dramatization of eternity. Included are accounts of the mechanism of the world, showing the machinery of the sun and moon in operation.

Enoch, according to these writings, was taken to Heaven, shown the great secrets of God and, over a 60-day period, wrote 366 books. Enoch is then returned to Earth for 30 days to give instruction to his sons and his children's children. After 30 days he was taken back to Heaven.

It appears that the pyramid may be a record of knowledge Enoch revealed to his sons. The pyramid could be a structure built by Enoch's sons to record for future generations a testimony and monument of the Lord and His secrets.

Inside the pyramid, there is a system of rising, descending, and horizontal passages linking a number of chambers with various dimensions, angles, and slopes recorded in stone.

The message is not in any language but is expressible in mathematics, the only true universal language. The revealed message is in terms of a mathematical code. The mathematical code connects to the words of scripture, recorded in the nineteenth and twentieth verses of Isaiah 19.

> *Isaiah 19:19, 20*
> 19. *In that day shall there be an altar to the Lord in the midst of the land of Egypt, and a pillar at the border thereof to the Lord.*
> 20. *And it shall be for a sign and for a witness unto the Lord of hosts in the land of Egypt: for they shall cry unto the Lord.*

In the Hebrew language, the letter symbols of the language are also the same symbols as numbers.

The 30 words of Isaiah 19:19 in Hebrew have a sum of 5,449. This is the total, numerically, of Isaiah 19:19. The distance between the north and the south poles, boring through the Earth, divided by 500 million equals 5,449. The number of pyramid inches from the base of the pyramid to the summit platform of the pyramid is 5,449. Simply a coincidence? I don't think so.

Two straight lines mark the point of beginning in the descending passage perpendicular to the floor of the descending passage. Recent astronomical research has revealed that these lines were aligned with the star Alcyone of the Pleiades in the constellation of Taurus the Bull at noon of the spring equinox or noon on March 21, 2141 BC.

This is the start of the prophecy and the messianic blue print that starts coming from 2141 BC.

Measuring from the starting point of 2141 BC and moving forward 688 pyramid inches or 688 years, we come to an ascending passage. The passage date is 1453 BC, the date of the beginning of the Exodus out of Egypt led by Moses. Three granite plugs block the entry of the ascending passage. These granite plugs symbolize the supernatural: the Passover, parting of the Red Sea, and giving of the Ten Commandments. The exact date is March 30, 1453 BC. The red granite of these plugs is only identical to the granite found on Mount Horeb.

The entry of the ascending passageway to the floor of the queen's chamber, or what is called the messianic triangle, is equal to April 1, 2 BC, which is the birth of Christ, measuring from the Exodus on March 30, 1453 BC. To the top of the messianic triangle, April 1, 33 AD come1485 pyramid inches or 1485 years.

The ascending passage increases by 77 inches on April 1, 33 AD, into the grand gallery.

Traveling up the ascending passage, there are three limestone girdle stones, which appear to be obstacles.

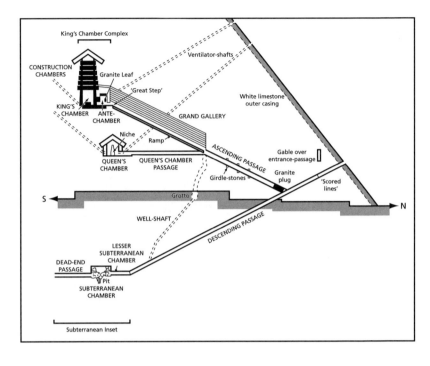

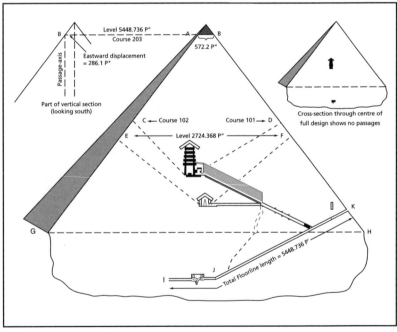

Markers precede each girdle stone: two on the west wall
and one on the east wall. They seem to signify that the
first and the third obstacles are separated from the middle
obstacle, as east is separated from west. The apparent dates
are seventh century BC for the first girdle and the third
century BC for the third girdle. The middle, or second,
girdle marked on the east wall is the fifth century BC.

The events of this historical time recorded in scripture are:

1. The first girdle = 722 BC. The ten northern tribes of
Israel are taken captive into Assyria for a 390-year siege.

2. The second girdle = 586 BC. The southern tribes of
Judah, Benjamin, and Livi are taken into Babylon. They
returned home in 536 BC and some with Esra in 458 BC to
their homeland.

3. The third girdle = 322 BC. The end of the 390-year
siege of the ten northern tribes. Alexander the Great
overthrew the Persian Empire.

The end of the ascending passage expands into the
grand gallery on April 1, 33 AD, the date that our Lord
Jesus was crucified on the cross. Marking back down the
ascending passage, the floor of the queen's chamber and
the floor of the descending passage meet at 2 BC,
signifying the birth of Christ.

Because of the angle of the ascending passage, meeting
with a horizontal passage at 2 BC, the date of 33 BC forms
a triangle by drawing a line from the ascending passage
to the floor of the queen's chamber. A line drawn from the
floor of the messianic triangle points directly to the city of
Bethlehem, the city where Jesus was born.

The ascending passage roof level expands on April 1, 33 AD, by 286.1 pyramid inches. The 286.1 pyramid inches figure is the measurement of eight things, possibly the sign of new beginnings.

1. The offset distance from the center of the north wall to enter the descending passage to the east.
2. This is also the distance by which the axis of the passage system lies to the east of the axis of the pyramid itself.
3. This is the same exact measurement that the ascending passage increases in the grand gallery of enlightenment.
4. This is the exact measurement of an open and empty coffin in the king's chamber.
5. This is the exact measurement of the missing headstone.
6. This is the exact measurement that Moses gave for the construction of the Ark of the Covenant.
7. The exact measurement from the messianic triangle to the wall shaft that leads to the subterranean chamber is exactly one-eighth of the 286.1.

This well shaft is the sign of Christ descending into hell to free the Old Testament saints while His Body spent three days in the rich man's tomb.

8. This is the exact measurement of the distance from the horizontal passage to the subterranean chamber and back up the descending passage to the well shaft, or way of escape, to the grand gallery.

Every place where the figure of 286.1 is measured in the pyramid, it seems to lead to a sign of enlightenment, resurrection, and life.

The pyramid inch is slightly different from the British inch. It is roughly the thickness of one-half of a single hair. This is the measurement used in building the Ark of the Covenant, the Tabernacle in the wilderness, Solomon's Temple, and the Temple that Ezekiel describes in Chapters 40 through 46 in his book.

This message of the pyramid is written in stone. The pyramid message is a universal message of enlightenment without labels, traditions, or doctrines.

PROPHETIC WORDS
OF ENCOURAGEMENT

When my personal relationship with the Lord began in 1968, my life changed drastically. When I was introduced to individuals who were blessed with the gift of prophecy and tongues, I was at first hesitant to worship the Lord with them. I had been programmed against these things. However, as I spent more time with them, I began to feel the presence of the Holy Spirit to a greater degree than I ever had before.

I wrote many of these prophecies down, and they have been a great encouragement to me over the years since the early 1980's. I believe the words spoken to me will be of great encouragement to many who reads them. So I will write them as the Lord spoke them to me and change only those to be directed to the reader. The Word of the Lord is alive, and will be spoken to anyone who reads these words and accepts them in faith as if spoken to you from the Lord. They will be a blessing to you (Zechariah 3:8, 9).

The Lord says that you are a pillar that can be counted upon. The Lord has you in the hollow of His hand. You will not vary from the path the Lord has chosen for you. Wait patiently upon the Lord, and you will live in the house that the Lord will build. The Lord has placed a seed of faith within your soul, and He has promised to open a way for you if you step out. The Lord is making a covenant with you that if you honor God, you will be glorified.

Many will fall by the wayside, but you are not to look back to pick anyone up. You are not to look back. You are to only look to the future.

All mountains set before you shall easily be removed with faith and trust in the Lord. Any words spoken against you are spoken against the Lord. You are not to rush into anything. If you wait upon the Lord, He will solve the problems for you.

The path of the Lord is straight, and there is no shadow of turning. When one says a penny's worth, you are to say *no;* for the Lord has promised and you shall receive.

The Lord wants you to know that He trusts you and asks you, "Can't you trust Me?" The Lord said, "Trust is like a trust fund." This trust will bring all things you need, and you will find what He has placed for you. You have received a treasure from the Lord and, if endorsed, it will open after you have walked the last mile.

You are not to humble yourself; for you are the head and not the tail. The Lord will do a work in you that you would not believe, even if He told you. The chair the Lord has chosen for you will fit no one else. The plan the Lord has laid out for you will fit no one else. The plan the Lord has for you is to be carried out by the mighty hand of God.

The Lord said, "Wisdom is yours for the taking. Wisdom and boldness have been given to you. The power and Spirit of God will lead, guide, and direct you."

The Lord will pick them up that are lowly and meek in spirit. The Lord has chosen and ordained you for a special work He has chosen. The Lord has brought you to a place where He can speak and lead you through a prophet. You will enter into a covenant with the Lord and do His will. The Lord has given you the gift of discerning of spirits.

Those that the Lord has chosen will walk together, talk together, and uphold one another. God's people are called from the lowly, but He will exalt them and they will not be ashamed. You are to be lowly and meek; for He said, "You are the servant of man."

*   *   *

God is no respecter of persons, and He acts according to each person's faith. If you don't believe, you don't receive. It's up to you whether these words have any meaning for you.

Even if one thousand come against you, they will be put to flight by the Lord. The Lord has put a hedge around you, and nothing can touch you. The Lord has set you on a path that He will provide. God's power comes over you, and you are overshadowed by an angel.

The Lord said that the hand held up will be drawn back. You are blessed this day; for God has counted you worthy.

All without the realm of trust, faith, hope, and charity will be put asunder.

You are to follow the leading of your heart and not your mind. If you lean on the Lord, He will show you the way. You will touch many, and many will follow after you.

Wherever you go, you may be blamed; and you may leave a heap of rubble behind, but the wind will blow it away. In this work many would slay you, but none will touch you. God will protect you. The Lord has ordained you for this work.

Your thoughts are given to you by the Lord. You are to go on your own thoughts and the leading of the Lord. You are set at the head and honored by the Lord, but it will be His conquest. The Lord will direct and give explicit instructions, and you will not vary from His written Word.

The Lord will seal you with His Spirit and with the new city of Jerusalem. You are to always check the scriptures for all things that have been spoken. Even through a prophet, the Lord will never vary from His written Word. God's words are pure, and they shall be adhered to. "The battle is not thine but Mine," sayeth the Lord. All God needs is a vessel that He can move around.

The Lord will lay within your right hand His treasures and you shall guard them. No thought will come to you contrary to the Lord's thoughts. The Lord will hedge you in and plant you solidly in the spirit with His grace. The Lord's hand is upon you, and His power over the Earth shall direct you.

Directions for the job the Lord has sent you on will be given one day at a time. Every morning you are to arise, praise the Lord, glorify His name, and see the works of the Lord.

*   *   *

Not listening to the Lord causes a heavy heart to ascend

upon His people. If God's people would listen to Him, many things could be straightened out. All who the Lord uses must be in strict obedience, or correction will come. The Lord dwells among His people and will guide them.

A rebellious spirit is worse than witchcraft.

If God's people hear His voice, He will lead them to the one He wants them to confer with. Following the Lord is a fine line that many cannot adhere to. All who love God's Word will know what He says and know what He means. All things are created by God and are for man. People will praise God and thank Him for the things He has laid before them. The path the Lord has chosen for you is laid out clearly, but it may be rough at times.

Some may come against you, but you are not to be disheartened; for you will be the overcomer. You will be the overcomer, and all that follow after you will be rewarded. The Lord has many things ahead for you, things to come in His time. The Lord's time is not your time, and your time is not His time. Things will be stopped if they come against God's time.

The Lord will do even more through you, but this well must be filled first. When this job is done, you are to look for another duty the Lord has for you. The Lord says you will travel for Him.

Each has a job He has chosen for them, and they must not step out on their own; for this only brings confusion. To clear the path, God will deal with each person in His own way.

You are to keep your heart and mind stayed upon the

Lord. The Lord says you have done well and stayed upon the path. You have thought things through, and your thinking has been excellent. The Lord said, "Did I not say I would show you the way? You are to walk day by day, and walk in peace."

The Lord shall prepare the words that you speak. The Lord said, "I have sent thee and they shall bow before you." The Lord said, "They shall not come against you as they thought, but they shall recede and draw back."

You are not to retrace your steps; for you have already covered this ground once. You are not to be encumbered with thoughts of others, but rely only upon your heart. Let no one say God has told them to tell you; for the Lord Himself has told you. The Lord praised you for being obedient to His Word. He said many get confused about His Word, but there is no confusion within you. The Lord said, "Many would come forth with false words, but you will not listen. You have accounted all things worthy, whatever I have spoken to you."

The Lord said that His Spirit is within the word that you have written. They are powerful, and they will touch many. You are to rely upon the Lord and pray each day for an accounting that will come. The raw edges are being filed off, and nothing will catch you unaware. All things shall be revealed by the Lord. You are not to look at the countenance, but know the vessel by the Spirit. Each is accountable to the Lord for all words that are spoken.

In a time of trouble, many shall come to you and speak things of their imagination.

The Lord said, "You are on an even keel, walking and talking to Me." The Lord will fill you in from time to time, and you are not to go without understanding. The Lord said He was at your command to fulfill all things which He has said. Honesty is of thee, and the countenance of yours shall reflect you to those that He would send you to. You are not to be controlled by anyone; for you are a child of the King. He said you have been strong, and power shall be released from you at the time of need.

WAKE UP TO UFO PHENOMENA

In reality the future is now, the finalization of God's preconceived plan of bringing all things under the control of His Son, Jesus Christ. God's plan in the creation of the human race was to create beings that could demonstrate His own personality of love and righteousness.

In order to have true love and true righteousness of the human will, there must be the desire and a choice by the free will of each man.

No one knows the history of the eons of time with God. The history of the spiritual world includes all the worlds, all matter, everything that exists. The knowledge of all mankind may be only a raindrop in the ocean compared to all that God has been, what God is, and what God will be.

Our knowledge is limited to only what we can perceive through our senses, intellect, mind, and spirit. The world's greatest thinkers and futurists only see a shadow of the future. And likewise, our greatest science and technology have only given us a shadow of history.

In our present understanding, we seem to continually discover changes in what we considered or understood as absolutes that could never be changed. We believe the scriptures to be true. We think we have an understanding of their meaning, and then we find new meaning and a change in our understanding of the truth that is written within this Word of God. It's like we find a new way or a new code of perception to a greater understanding.

Who can say with certainty what existed on our tiny speck of God's creation, planet Earth? Or what existed a thousand years ago or even ten billion years ago?

How many forms of humanity and other forms of life may have been recycled upon this Earth? How can anyone say there is only evolution or that there is only creation? There is room for the reality of every creative thought in God's plan, but there is no room for any limitations.

Any preconceived realities can leave us open for deception in what lies ahead. In the present cycle of God's plan upon this Earth, He has given us a survival plan that will lead to peace, joy, and love beyond our present understanding.

This is the state of everlasting life. This survival plan may be summarized in the following statements:

1. Accept Him as your loving creator.
2. Accept Jesus, His Son, as the Lord whom He sent to die in order that the curse of sin may be taken from you.
3. Learn to hear His voice and submit to the urging of that inner voice.
4. Have faith by believing God loves you and is in control of all things.
5. Know that you were created for a purpose.
6. Know that God wants you to be a part of His plan.

7. By seeking, listening, and being obedient,
    you will be given the power to overcome
    all obstacles.

The Bible gives us a shadow of things that appear to be taking place. The prophet, Daniel, interpreted the dream of King Nebuchadnezzar while the people of Judah were being held in Babylon. This dream was the statue of a man made of a head of gold, a chest of silver, thighs of brass, legs of iron, and feet and toes made of iron and clay.

The interpretation is an overview of future rulers from the time of Daniel and Nebuchadnezzar. The time from the gold head to the end of an age is described in symbolic form. The very end of the age is described in the feet and the toes, the very time we are in fact living in today. The toes are made of a mixture of iron and miry clay.

The possible meaning of the iron and the clay may need to be re-examined in the reality of our present times.

Today, it appears that we are about to be invaded by forces from other dimensions and from other worlds. We have all heard stories of flying saucers and alien beings. There are many stories of people being abducted that seem to be related to signs left in fields, known as crop circles, and the farm animals that are found mutilated with their blood drained and sex organs removed.

The Bible gives plenty of evidence of the reality of alien beings.

The time is now for all believers to be awakened to this reality. It appears that an encounter is about to take place that will frighten and confuse most of the population upon the Earth. This will be a test of everyone's belief system because we have been taught and believed in a traditional understanding of all things, including the Bible, that these beings did not exist or were not for us to be concerned about.

The theme of the Bible is the battle between spiritual forces created by God.

The angels were disrupted by a power struggle when Lucifer, an angel of great beauty and great power, became jealous and tried to overthrow his own creator. He tried to take the position of Christ and become equal with God.

To settle this according to God's own righteous law, rather than destroy Satan, He allowed the powers of darkness and evil to tempt God's created beings and bring them to a point of being able to choose between following the forces of evil or righteousness. The rulership of God's creation is the reward. We have a choice whether to enter into hell and damnation or to enter the state of eternal life.

The Bible tells us that Satan and all his followers will be cast into a lake of fire and darkness forever.

The Bible never gives us a complete story, only what we need to know in understanding certain points. Besides the angels, Jesus said there were principalities and powers that humans were not aware of.

We don't know how many forms of living beings there may be under their own rulership. It may be only a few, or it may be billions. And we don't know whether there are other civilizations on physical planets, or how many celestial or spiritual beings in nature there may be. It appears that Satan has control of at least a few of these principalities and powers.

It appears that some of these physical principalities are what we call UFO's or beings in the flying saucers. There are other principalities of the demonic nature that are spirits or part of the celestial. Their nature seems to be to dwell within or take over or control the will of humanity.

The Lord is in absolute control of all of these forces, and the Bible tells us that Satan is the accuser of the brethren even before God's throne. So some evil forces have access to certain parts of the heavens. Others are bound in the inner Earth. The Bible speaks of evil spirits bound up over Persia as well as the evil Prince of Tyre and the demonic forces over Babylon.

The Bible warns us that, besides all the forces of evil upon the Earth that we see today, a whole new force of evil is to be released upon the Earth at the closing of the age in which this generation is living.

The Bible tells us that Satan can take many forms. He can be a snake or dragon or an angel of light, and I'm sure anything in between. It appears that some evil forces have the ability to materialize into the physical from the spiritual reality.

Throughout history, we see that Satan has tried to pervert the forces of creation by perverting sex. We see this in the days of Noah when fallen angels had sex with the women upon Earth, creating a race of giants. We also see the perverted sex that caused God to destroy Sodom and Gomorrah.

Today we also see the evidence of sexual organs being taken from thousands of animal mutilations. And the abducted people say that sperm samples were taken from them while on board space ships. Some people claim to having had sex with aliens and later being shown their offspring, half-human and half-alien. They seem to be creating some type of inter-dimensional race of beings.

I believe that Daniel gives us insight to what is happening.

> *Daniel 2:41-43*
> 41. *And whereas thou sawest the feet and toes, part of potters clay, and part of iron, the kingdom shall be divided; but there shall be in it of the strength of iron for as much as thou sawest the iron mixed with miry clay.*
> 42. *And as the toes of the feet were part iron, and part of clay, so the kingdom shall be partly strong, and partly broken.*
> 43. *And whereas thou sawest the iron mixed with clay, they shall mingle themselves with the seed of men: but they shall not cleave one to another, even as iron is not mixed with clay.*

Prophetic teachers talk about the European common market recently formed as being the fulfillment of the ten-toed kingdom spoken of by Daniel. We need to remember that the Roman Empire included more than the European nations. Also included was Iraq, part of Iran, part of Saudi Arabia, Egypt, Libya, Tunisia, Jordan, Syria, and Turkey. There was the western portion of the Roman Empire, and there was the Eastern portion of the Roman Empire.

So Daniel's prophecy could be accurately fulfilled if there was a combination of five western European nations and five Middle Eastern nations that were part of the original Roman Empire.

THEY SHALL MINGLE THEMSELVES WITH THE SEED OF MEN (Daniel 2:43).

This seems to be a union between human and nonhuman beings. Could this be the reason for the taking of sex organs in the animal mutilations? Could this be the reason for the taking of sperm samples? Are they performing their own form of genetic engineering for their own purposes?

The scripture gives further evidence of what may be taking place in the Spiritual Realm that will also manifest itself in physical reality here on the Earth. We see a connection between the Branch, the man-child, and the stone cut out of the mountain without hands. All three of these are symbols that describe the same time and events spoken of by Daniel, Isaiah, Jeremiah, and John in the Book of Revelation. There now appears to be a war taking place in Heaven that will soon be concluded. We see this foretold in Revelation.

> *Revelation 12:11*
> *11. And there appeared a great wonder in heaven; a woman clothed with the sun, and the moon under her feet, and upon her head a crown of 12 stars.*

The woman seems to be the body of Christ—the bride whose time has come. The sun is her purity being clothed in the light of Jesus Christ—the light of the world. The 12 stars seem to have several meanings.

1. The message of the Zodiac pointing to Christ that the three wise men recognized by coming to Bethlehem.
2. The 12 apostles with Christ.
3. The reuniting of the ten lost tribes of Israel with Judah.

Revelation 12:2-5
2. *And she being with child cried, travailing in birth, and pained to be delivered.*
3. *And there appeared another wonder in heaven; and behold a great red dragon, having seven heads and ten horns, and seven crowns upon its heads.*

The birth of the man-child is the birth of the Branch, the 144,000 spoken of in the seventh chapter of Revelation. This is the spiritual army of God, manifested in His overcomers on the Earth today. They defeat all forces of evil, alien or otherwise, with the word of their testimony, having no fear of death and by the power of the blood of the Lamb of God.

Satan is the great red dragon having seven heads and ten horns. This seems to be his method of operation in the Spiritual Realm that he is trying to bring forth upon the Earth. A reflection of his rulership is seen in the principalities and powers of the aliens invading us in UFO's.

4. *And his tail drew the third part of the stars of heaven, and did cast them to the Earth: and the dragon stood before the woman which was ready to be delivered, for to devour her child as soon as it was born.*

This may be a part of the UFO phenomena we see building up to a confrontation, an invasion upon Earth of the forces of evil.

5. *And she brought forth a man-child, who was to rule all nations with a rod of iron: and her child was caught up unto God, and to his throne.*

This is not a physical birth, but a spiritual birth, of the people upon the Earth. Being caught up to His throne is the spiritual power of those, abiding in Christ, who enter into the joint venture between Heaven and Earth. They are totally abiding in Christ and letting Him lead and direct in the war against the forces of evil. The birth is spiritual, and the being caught up is also spiritual. That is what the birth is all about—letting Christ be the head. At the time we see all of this happening, at the invasion of the extraterrestrial aliens, we also see the ten European nations being formed. *The mingling of nonhumans mix with the seed of men.* And beyond all the evil, there is something wonderful also happening at the same time.

Daniel 2:44
44. *And in the days of these kings shall the God of heaven set up a kingdom, which shall never be destroyed; and the*

kingdom shall not be left to other people, but it shall break in pieces and consume all these kingdoms, and it shall stand forever.

Most scholars have erred in using this verse to state that the stone is Christ, and that He will break up and defeat the anti-christ and his kingdom when He returns.

IN, not *after*, is the key to understanding. *IN the days* that you see this happening means *at the same time*. It does not mean at the end or the conclusion or after. It means *at the same time*.

This stone is the Kingdom of God, made up of His people, who come together into one body without any denominational or religious barriers. We are given power when we learn to submit and let Jesus Christ be the head. Then we become the forces that will defeat all the kingdoms of the world upon the Earth.

Daniel 2:45

45. *For as much as thou sawest that the stone was cut out of the mountain without hands, and that it brake in pieces the iron, the brass, the clay, the silver, and the gold; the great God hath made known to the king what shall come to pass hereafter: and the dream is certain, and the interpretation is sure.*

In previous chapters, I have explained the anointing described by Isaiah for the body of Christ when we come into unity as a single voice, all of one accord. Jesus Himself spoke of this Branch in the New Testament, explaining the power and authority of the Branch totally submitted to Himself, the Vine. The stone cut out of the mountain without hands that breaks in pieces and consumes the world's kingdoms is the same body of Christ that He uses to establish His kingdom. This is the calling of you and me of this generation. Isaiah explains in Isaiah 10:26 that *The Lord will do something in the future very similar to what the Lord did through Moses when he lifted up His rod over Egypt.* In the very next verse, Isaiah 10:27, Isaiah explains that this will be the anointing that will break the yoke from off thy neck. This implies the release of all bondage.

THOUGHTS ABOUT THE STUDY OF PROPHECY

I will first state what I believe may be possibilities when the rapture and the war of Armageddom may take place. The sequences of events are based upon what I feel the Lord has revealed to me and by the study of scriptures.

It seems that in the end, events sometimes appear as if we are entering the Garden of Eden by going backwards. For example, after the fall of Adam, the first generation lived nearly 1,000 years. Now it appears that the people of this generation entering into the Kingdom will live life spans covering the 1,000-year reign. Maybe the language of creation is similar to the language of restoration.

It appears the rapture will be a mid-tribulation period rapture. There is pretty strong evidence in my mind that there will be two raptures. The first will be at the seventh trumpet when the kingdoms of this Earth become the Kingdoms of God after the first half of the tribulation period. This will evidently be the event when the Lord appears in the clouds with the saints, we rise up to meet Him, and we are changed in the twinkling of an eye. The second will be at the end of the millennial reign, just prior to the bowl judgments, when the plagues will cover the entire Earth, rather than the one-third of the Earth judged during the trumpet judgments.

The war of Ezekiel 38 and 39 seems to bring forth the

1,000-year reign, and the war of Armageddon will be at the end of the millennial period, after Satan is released.

The time period of a short time may be a few days, weeks, months, or years in God's timetable. In God's time, earth's history is only six days because 1,000 years of Earth time is only one day in the Lord's time.

It seems that the 144,000 are about to be revealed for this generation. They appear to be the overcomers, and they appear under several titles, including the Branch, the man-child, and the man on the white horse of Revelation 6:1, 2.

The scriptures are written in a way that they will always be relevant. It seems each generation gets a new understanding of scripture as new revelations are revealed. As one reads and gets understanding, there is a facet at some future time in another generation when truths come out, and another facet or portion of prophecy seems to be fulfilled.

For this reason, it is a great mystery to be solved, or a great puzzle to be put together, over and over again as new revelations and meanings are revealed.

In the study of prophecy, we must always be sure that we go in a straight line. If we have to change our understanding of one of our precepts of symbols we use in interpretation, then something is wrong. We always must go in a straight line. A truth is eternal and never changes.

Isaiah 28: 9-13

9. *Whom shall he teach knowledge? And whom shall he make to understand doctrine? Them that are weaned from the milk, and drawn from the breasts.*

10. *For precept must be upon precept, precept upon precept; line upon line; here a little, and there a little;*

11. *For with stammering lips and another tongue will he speak to his people.*

12. *To whom he said, This is the rest wherewith ye may cause the weary to rest: and this is the refreshing: yet they would not hear.*

13. *But the word of the Lord was unto them precept upon precept; line upon line, line upon line; here a little and there a little; that they might go, and fall backward, and be broken, and snared, and taken.*

PART III

THE WORK OF THE SPIRIT

When we turned over the new millennium on January 1, 2000, something happened spiritually. I sensed a new release of the Spirit of the Lord upon the Earth. On January 1, there was change. Once, I would fast and pray for several days to hear the Lord speak. Since the dawning of the new millennium, my sensitivity has greatly been increased by the Lord, and I am able to go at any time into that quiet place and communicate with the Lord. I want to make it clear that I am not entirely sure that every word is of the Lord. But, again, I present these words as my present understanding of what I believe the Lord is telling me. I do not claim to be anyone other than a listener wanting to share what I believe I have heard spoken to me from the Lord.

It is not as if I can close my eyes and begin praying, and then the Lord speaks to me in the way that you might speak to another person. At times I am not sure what it is the Lord is revealing to me. The thoughts, which I believe to be of the Lord, come in fragments. I can sometimes sit down at my computer keyboard and begin typing without being fully aware of what I am typing until I have finished. I do not claim to be a prophet. Following is my understanding of what the Lord has chosen to reveal to me through prophetic teachings. They are dated according to the days that I received them from the Lord and are written in a way that expresses how they came from the Lord Himself directly to me.

January 1, 2000

The world is not coming to an end, but the Kingdom is beginning. The events of September supercede or overwhelm the other events on my calendar. The judgments have been rendered and decided. The notice of execution is being rendered. The notice of annulment of debt has gone forth. The redeemed have been brought forth. It is a victory of redemption. The victory of reclaiming all that has been taken. The righteous have proclaimed the victory, the world has gone forth, and the Kingdom is at hand. Wake up My people to the fact of impending events. You are to release My people of what they dread— fear of destruction. The Kingdom is at hand, and the victory is ours. The millennial reign has begun and will be proclaimed to the ends of the Earth.

Lord, I was going to ask You to show me the future. Lord, You are the future.

In your mind, you have chosen to be invisible, allowing Me to be visible in your being. The way of magnification is the growth process. By giving Me your will, you have decided to become whatever I desire you to become. By keeping your thoughts upon Me, you become like Me. Your prayers guide your thoughts to the Kingdom. The Kingdom becomes part of you and you become part of the Kingdom. This is the process of submission to My will. I then take you in or absorb you in My thought process— the heavenly consciousness.

We are all then of one mind and accord. The power of

the Kingdom is the manifestation of the glory of God in the image of each member. Visualize the chief cornerstone as the largest stone or the smallest grain of sand, regardless of size, having the same illumination, magnificence, and glory—each one magnifying the others. The smallest becomes the total concentration of the Kingdom. The entire Kingdom is in one grain of sand. The entirety of the Kingdom becomes the manifestation of each grain to a stone and then to the Kingdom. This is an all-in-one and one-in-all process. Each becomes what it individually wants to become with the Kingdom becoming the entirety of the desire of each individual. The importance is of unity, of being all of one mind and accord. It is important that Christ be in each life and each life be in Christ.

Abide in me and I in you. As the Branch cannot bear fruit of itself, except it abide in the vine, no more can ye, except ye abide in me (John 15:14).

I will teach you, My son, and you will teach My people the wonder of communications that goes beyond the planet or the galaxies of the universe. This communication is the creator of all things.

In the beginning was the Word—the Word of creation. I was the Word and I am still the Word and I am still the Word of creation. I am in you, and you are in Me. I am your word, and you speak My Word. The word of truth prevails. It is eternal and everlasting without change.

You are created by your own word, and you become what your thoughts and words speak. You become faithful by speaking faith. You become righteous by speaking righteously—just as you become fearful by speaking of fear and you become an untrusted liar by speaking a lie.

Whatever you want or whatever you want to become, you must speak. The Word is like a seed that grows. You can see this creation and evolution in every growth process. When you abide in Me and I abide in you, we are the same thought and the same word. This is more than just working in harmony. It is I working in you and you working in Me. You become one with Me as I am one with the Father.

The power of your word must be spoken wisely. The fear of the Lord is the beginning of wisdom. Becoming wise is abiding in Christ. Abiding in Christ is being one in Christ. The will must be willed to God's perfect will. We are building a chain, link by link, of perfect communication. Each link is without any limitation connected to all wisdom, power, and glory. Picture this as magnetism. My Spirit communicates not only to each stone, but also through each stone linked to all the others. Each personality is enlightened and energized in perfect love and perfect harmony, like that perfect city—the holy Jerusalem, the bride, the Lamb's wife.

The communication has begun. You are beginning to see the light of My Word. The light is electrical in energy. The Word became the light of the world, but the world knew it not. You have walked the mile of independence— the mile of freedom from the influences of the world riches.

You have struggled, but you have made it to the safety of the net—the net of righteousness. Now I am holding you securely from the flames of the unrighteous. The world has seen the gulf between us. They are envious and want to cross over, but they don't know how. You are to toss them a rope to hold on to. You are to invest the treasures of the Kingdom. Walk in the way that I have shown you to walk. The way has been made clear. The entryway into the Kingdom you have already entered. The way is being made for you to stand as a pillar of encouragement.

The glory of the Earth's finances will behold and declare the glory of the Kingdom. This will be a day of atonement with sin offerings flowing into the Kingdom. The righteous have walked the path of pure gold. You have been put on this path—the never-ending path in and through the Kingdom. Watch the way I have chosen to serve you, My son.

The Word has been made clear for understanding. You will teach the values of proper understanding. Your resistance has decreased, and you will be able to move around the obstacles placed before you. Yes, I am the way, the truth, and the life. I will show you the way I have chosen for you.

Whatever happens is foretold, and it will happen just as it is foretold. Understanding the meaning of the posted prophetic signs is important. The signs of distress are most prominent, just as are road signs or stop lights warning you to avoid danger. The other signs or directions and the proper lanes to turn or to exit at the proper speed are meant to make the trip safe and enjoyable, thus avoiding the dangers.

This is how you are to read My prophetic road map. The ways are marked clearly, the way of safety as well as the way of destruction. There are also unexpected storms that sometimes endanger the trip.

If My people are told the signs and weather conditions of the world, they may choose the way, the truth, and the life by abiding in Me. Let Me be the driver through the times of trouble. My people are to submit by faith and trust in My guidance. I will deliver My people. I am a good driver as well as a good shepherd for My sheep.

January 3, 2000

The problems of yesterday are gone. Walk arounds are taking place. The problems are being taken care of with Y2K. What have you been doing worrying? My son, the way has been made clear. You have already traveled the road of destruction. The feeble have fallen, but you have endured. The way has been made clear now for you to travel in peace.

The way has been made clear, and you will be filled with joy as you go. You have been working in anticipation of delightful days ahead. The other side of the coin says it will happen soon. The event of the centuries approaches—the Millennial Reign of Christ.

You have walked the walk and talked the talk of independent thinkers. The way of understanding is understood by you. You have evolved as a master of My Word.

The world wants to know about the beginning and the ending of this era. The way has been made clear for you to show the world the way and by what means I work upon the Earth.

January 4, 2000

A new day is beginning. A new dawn will soon be here. I have given you a new beginning. The way is not well traveled, but it is clear. I have shown you the way, and you won't be alone. I will always be at your side.

The awakening has begun. The man-child is coming forth. The Branch has matured and is bearing fruit. Wake up the people. The world revival has begun. Be ready. There will be a coming forth from all nations. It will be as though a dam has burst as My people rush to find a glimmer of light, a lost hope.

Wait upon the March winds. The travel of time is near and will be made clear. The molecular structure permits the destruction and construction of flesh and bone by the spirit. The spirit attuned by the soul to the Holy Spirit becomes one with My Spirit. My Spirit is My will and My soul. My soul and Spirit are inseparable. Through the new birth, My Spirit becomes one with your spirit.

When you become a true spiritual being, your soul becomes one with your spirit, totally submissive to the spirit's leading. The linkage is your soul to spirit, your spirit to My Spirit, soul, and will. My desires and your desires are the same. All limitations are eliminated. We have perfect communication. We commune together, so your will is being done through Me and My will is being done through you. This submitting to My will becomes binding of our wills jointly. We share all our joint experiences and plans through your physical mind and body. Everything, such as healings, miracles, even time travel and spiritual transportation, will be used.

You have been doing the work of the Lord by worshipping the Lord your God. I have been rebuilding upon your words, rebuilding the Earth. The work of building My Kingdom is our joint venture. It has been said that the prayers of men move the hands of God. When I was asked how to pray, I prayed, "Thy kingdom come, thy will be done on Earth as it is in Heaven." Every answered prayer is My will. My eyes are constantly upon everything concerning everyone on Earth. The Earth is the training ground for My people to bring My people to a point where receiving answered prayers is as easy as breathing, even subconsciously.

Prayer is communion with Me, both on a conscious and an unconscious or spiritual level. The prayer lines are clear when there is no sin, no worry, no anxiety. Perfect faith is perfect peace. The most perfect prayer is the simple prayer, the Lord's prayer. This allows Me to bless you with what you want and need at your deepest and greatest spiritual desire. You will be taken care of. I have promised you that.

You are still being prepared for the work I have laid before you. All at once, the world will know the work and the mission for all My people. You have enjoyed the sorrows of your past. Did I not say count it a joy when you fall into persecution? You have seen the growth and the power you were given when you were under stressful situations. You have gained strength and wisdom that can be counted on whenever you need it.

Your words of truth will prevail upon the truth. All errors and untruths will be proven. It is like you are panning for gold as you seek My still, small voice and sift everything through the water of My Word. The treasures are found as you wash and sift through every word. Your words spoken in revealing My true treasures will bring riches to many.

Wait upon the Lord, and He will give you strength. You have waited, and I have given you strength that you are not yet aware of. The joy of knowing that you are in My will and that I am watching over everything that concerns you is shown in your quiet, still faith. Waiting upon Me to move shows Me that I have you in the palm of My hand, and you know that all is well. Messengers will be coming soon. The news will be good. Study the objectives. You will be able to influence them. Wait upon Me, My son. I have made your choice, and it is the best.

Be courageous, My son. The Word of the Lord has gone forth. You are to receive the blessings of the Lord. You will feed My people with finances of the Lord. The world will know that the glory of the Lord has come forth. The faith of a mustard seed has prospered. It has grown into an exceedingly great tree. The worth of the fruit cannot be calculated. The production will continually grow.

Worthy is the Lamb of God. He has given beyond our dreams. He has provided us a kingdom of abundance. The workers have gone forth in the name of the Lord. The Spirit of the Lord has prevailed to call My people to action. He has dispersed the angels on their assignments. Who are the chosen to wait upon the Lord? Be still, so very still. The Lord is in control. He will speak, and you will hear. You must trust that strange thought that was not your own. Let your heart overflow with praise for the Lord. He knows everything about you, and He will direct your path perfectly.

* * *

Yea, I say unto you the way has been made clear. You are to wait on the wings of foundational truth. The weight of enlarged understanding will give balance to their objectives. The work of progression has been completed. You have understood by the ways and the means that I proceed to move. The entire international community of nations will proceed to enlarge their appetite for spiritual enlightenment. The wonderment of traditional spiritual values has penetrated into the minds of the Far East. The indignation has ceased. The time of revival has come.

My Spirit will proceed to do a new thing. You will see the end of the entire civil unrest you now see upon the Earth. Look at the Biblical events of the past as signs and prophecies of the future—as if human history was on a film played in reverse. How would it look? As we see the mistakes, we would go right to the beginning of each changing event in world history. Each change of the world would be the result of a decision by one man, and that decision was the result of a thought from the heart of a man. Thoughts and words become decisions.

As a man thinks, he changes the world. A thought becomes an action that causes a chain reaction that changes the world. Today, the world is the product of thoughts and actions of all humanity. Think how the world might be if Abraham had not been obedient to leave his family and go to a new land. Every nation and every person upon Earth are leading a life changed by that one decision of Abraham's obedience.

Now visualize how the Kingdom of God will become when all My people submit to My will in obedience to Me. You see, self-will leads to many perceived successes that cause disharmony or even hostility to others upon the Earth. Only through submission and obedience to the spirit of life in Christ Jesus will the Earth's potential be reached.

I have given mankind everlasting life. Whether you see this as one life or several reincarnations. Men should think in terms well beyond what seems far off. How will your thoughts and actions today effect the new millennium or even the next ten million? You will be there to see for yourselves.

The creative thinking comes from Me, your creator. You have learned the secret of totally submitting your will and mind to Me. Your mind does not become empty because I fill it with treasures.

You will see the shifting of the sun soon. The atmospheres will change. The air will be full of lightning and thunder. There will be three days of darkness. This marks the beginning of the count down to Armageddon.

The moon will tilt and sway to the right. You have been

used to summer weather, and you will receive more of it. The morning after will be devastating to My people. Many will die of shock. You will be able to help many; for you are prepared mentally and physically.

The Earth will rumble and roar. The evening sky will be ablaze with fire and lightning. The entire Earth will be like a war zone. Every mountain will be moved, but My people will be safe.

I have moved mountains, but I have kept My people safe. You will not understand this until you see it. You are prepared. Make no moves to prepare. I will move mountains to save My people. They will know that I am the Lord their God.

January 6, 2000

This will be the great attention getter. They will see the great destruction, but they will also see the great miracles I have done to save My people. Many more throughout the world will turn to Me.

The day has come, My son: the day of bewilderment for My people; the day of restitution; the day that I have redeemed My people to their glory. My people will no longer be satisfied with what the world has to offer. Their hearts will be opened unto Me. I will satisfy their desires of love. They will know that I love and care for them. The work of the house has begun. The whole house of Israel will be restored. The paving of the streets is now being done. The shaking to bring all the parts together has begun. The entire structure will be completed soon.

This is the highway of reconstruction. The waiting is done. The travel is now. The bones must solidly be put together. You have the power to couple the joints together. The house of Israel is now waiting upon you, and your waiting has ended. You must go now. My Temple will be visible for all to see in its magnificence.

Yea, I have said unto you the way would be made clear. You are ready, and you are prepared. Go with confidence of My presence and strength with you. You have believed, and I have been faithful to your faith. The trust fund has worked for both of us. My Father has given you to Me, and I have ordained and anointed you for this special work. You have worn the garments of praise and the robe of righteousness given to you by My Father.

Many will wonder why I have chosen you out of all those that the Father has given Me. The men of renown have asked Me. I have given you a meek spirit of quiet strength, not visible to many about you. This is the faith needed to stand on your own. You have withstood the pressures, asking only My perfect will. This has allowed the flames of refinement to burn a little hotter and a little longer.

Yea, the Word of the Lord has come forth. You have been called to this purpose. You have been called and ordained for a marvelous and a mighty work. The world will be shaken, but you will be in the palm of My hand. The world will not cease nor end. But the world system *will* be turned over. My people will be raised up, and they will rule disobedience to My standard with a rod of iron. My Word and My law shall go forth from Jerusalem. Jerusalem is My dwelling place. Zion is My home forever; it will never be moved. Zion is My Holy Mountain.

January 7, 2000

You have been working on a detailed description of the future. The understandings are unaware to the people trying to figure out the end times. The keys of the Kingdom are written within these words. You have understanding of some, and some I have withheld from your understanding. The reading of the Word of God reveals new words written within the meaning of the old.

You have been waiting on Me, My son. I have been choosing the delights of the day, and I am ready to show you the answers to your questions. The answers are written. I have shown you, and you have understood the meaning. The sequence alters the understanding. You have unraveled the truth of My Word. The unraveling needs to be ironed out. The sentences and understanding will be smooth when the notes in your mind are revealed in your written word. You have understanding that you are not aware of.

The ancients of days are recorded in your mind. The ancients of days are the records of your past. You have traveled this road of the past, and you will travel it again in the future. The beginnings and the endings are the same. The only difference is the environment. The ages are different, but the spiritual reality is the same. The thoughts, the joys, and the frustrations are revealed in the lives of many generations.

The great wonder is whether they are able to recognize the different choices that need to be made. You have chosen the major error of many. But you will prevail if the matters are proven according to the way I have shown you. The test is if the event does occur. If not, the objectives were accomplished anyway.

Faith has a way of becoming reality by realizing the event has already happened. All you have to do is believe, and it will be revealed unto you as experience in your life. The act of faith relies on knowing the events of tomorrow. I reveal the words to you. You believe, and I reveal the truth in reality. The waves of truth flow in and out of your mind on a very low conscious level.

In order to understand these words, you must know the way that I reveal My will to My people. They believe the truth when they believe the words that I put in their hearts. This is the confidence that I can give to believe the truth. If the confidence is there, believe. If the confidence is not there, do not believe.

I have told you the way of knowing the truth. The way and the truth are the same when you have the confidence. The truth provides the way. Believe, and you shall receive. You have the confidence and believe all that I have revealed to you. The time has come for you to see the reality, and I will show you the truth of what you believe in reality.

*   *   *

The way I have made mobility of My people is by moving investment banking into areas of non-collateral loans. The lenders are realizing the difference of using memberships of My servers—the people of My making, the people who love and serve Me. They have allowed the management of My people, by their own self-discipline, to be of benefit to the lenders.

The financing of the Kingdom is coming unto them in a way they did not expect. The event will occur soon, and you will see the finances of the Kingdom flow in to you. Fee simple properties will be purchased by non-collateral loans. You will be endeavored to buy and sell as you please. The only requirement will be to release My people from the oppression of their present lenders. This will be fee simple and will benefit My people. You will be adjusting the relationships you have. The evenings will not be lonely, and the days will not be long. All your expectations will be satisfied.

My people will become the management enterprise of the world. You will be moving My people to their desired locations and living conditions. You are now unaware of the context in which I am saying this, but you will see the eventual fall of Babylon beyond the Jordan River, the real Babylon. The entire universe is filled with My glory, and I have chosen you to serve this glory to My people. You will see the mountains move at your presence. The faith of a mustard seed has paid off for you. You are receiving the benefits now. If you see the unraveling of businesses, you will know that I have not chosen them for our enterprise.

The wisdom of men is not for bending the truth as they have. The lies they tell have resulted in the development of enterprises that will not work. And I have chosen to be the fall guy. You know that I mean they will fall and I will be the guy they hate. I, the Lord thy God, have spoken this. I will be revealed to My people, and they will know that I am the God of thy fathers. You have spoken it, and I will prove it in truth.

January 8, 2000

I have chosen you, My son, and I have chosen your family. Did I not choose the sons and daughters of Abraham as well? Did I not protect Lot, Abraham's nephew? I will do the same for you, My son, and I promised to restore to you all that had been lost or stolen. That also relates to relationships. You have spoken the truth in recognizing that Satan cast upon you. That evil has been stamped under My feet and will not appear again. You have the true word of Me, the Lord your God—of Me, Jesus Christ, the one who came in the flesh.

The physical redemption of My people has begun. They are being redeemed from their bonds, that is, the selective service of the laws of governments and, most of all, from the bondage of sin.

You have spoken this in matters of extraordinary spiritual warfare. Your words have prevailed, and the enemy has been bound from the planned invasions upon My people. You have proclaimed and have not denied the Word of God, the most powerful force upon the Earth. The unity of the body of Christ is mounting a monumental power structure for the Kingdom of God. The way of the king has been known unto My people.

The king, David, My anointed one, was a king of My choice. The others after Solomon were kings of the people they ruled. Solomon was a ruler of oppression to My people. I gave him wisdom, and he failed to follow wisdom's choice of the use of wisdom. Wisdom will gain the goals of the beholder of wisdom. Success of building his own kingdom was Solomon's choice of his own will.

I have also given you, as yet unseen, wisdom. With your wisdom, you have given your will to Me, the Lord your God, to do My will in building My Kingdom.

The wisdom of God is the wisdom of your choice, My will over your will. You have become the wisest of men. The wise will see and recognize the wisdom of your heart. They will see My stamp of approval.

The way has been made for the wise to follow the wise. The trail will be long, and it will contain all the power of the wise. The waiting has ended, and yet you are still waiting on the wise choice of knowing before going. You have been receiving instruction on My Word, and I have mentioned many things you do not understand fully. You are still wondering what to do and how to do it.

I have spoken to you before, but you have not heard the call to arms. Move only when the cloud moves, and place ahead of every move a sanctuary just as the armies of the twelve tribes did in the tenth chapter of Numbers.

After reading this, my understanding was: The cloud will be moving soon, and you will see the red ring around the sun, the ring of authority that I will cast upon your finger. You have spoken the words of truth. The declaration of independence has been enforced. You have spoken and declared the independence of My people by declaring that you are the chosen generation to bring forth the Kingdom of God.

Keep your mind stayed upon Me, and I will show you

great and mighty things—the things I decided before the beginning of time when the world began.

I was planning a great holiday of festivities for My people that My Father had given Me. My trusted friend turned against Me, and became My enemy and the enemy of all My people. He tried deceitfully to use all the glory and the power I had given him against Me.

One of the most trusted sons of God turned Heaven upside down by rejecting My love and deceitfully turned one-third of the angels against Me. Everything started from the energy of My spoken Word. From nothing, everything that is, or will be, came forth. The Word was My plan that also included every thought and every action of all creation of physical matter and spiritual energy. The wiles of the devil were and still are never a surprise to Me. The end is already finished in that original Word. I am the Alpha and Omega. There is no end to spiritual energy made up of the life you know as the spirit.

The spirit has no limitations or boundaries beyond My Word. All things are subject to My Word. The spirit is the river of life, the pure water flowing from the Father. Through My Word, all the elements of all creation are washed by the living water and take shape according to the original plan of My Word. If My Word was placed in the form of a book to be understood by men, all the space of all the planets and galaxies would not hold the pages. The story of creation and time is but one small chapter in My book.

The element of surprise scares My people and Satan

uses this to scare My people, but there is no surprise to Me. Satan had his role as a part of that river of life. His portion will never see death, but will burn in fire and brimstone forever. The spiritual followers of Heaven you call fallen angels and demons are called the Host of Heaven. They stand outside My door pretending to be angels of light to usher My people through the gate with many paths that anyone may choose. But the path is very narrow, and I am the true gate. Can you now grasp the meaning?

In the beginning was the Word and the Word was with God and the Word *was* God. In Him was life and the light was of men. And the Word was made flesh and dwelt among you. My people are born again, not of corruptible seed, but incorruptible by the Word of God, which liveth and abideth in you forever.

If My Word is life, creation, and light and if I am that Word and if I dwell inside of My people, why are they not creators? Why are they not givers of life and givers of light? My Word is all of this and more, but the Word acts only according to My will. The secrets and powers of the Kingdom were given to My people when I explained how they should pray. I said, "Your Father knoweth what things ye have need of before ye ask Him."

After this manner thereof pray:

Our Father which art in Heaven. Hallowed be thy name. Thy kingdom come. Thy will be done, on Earth, as it is in heaven. Give us this day, our daily bread. Forgive us our debts as we forgive our debtors. Lead us not into temptation, but deliver us from evil. For thine is the kingdom and the power and the glory forever.

Think of the power of My Word spread among My people. All of this power is Mine to give, the power of creation out of nothing, the power to give life to the whole universe. I'm spreading all My power among all My people to have a new Heaven and a new Earth under the power and the authority of My Word operating in and through My people by My Spirit. Do you understand the power of the Word that I have given to you, My son? My Word spoken through your words when you are abiding in Me. Did I not say, "Ask what you will and it will be done unto you?"

Now visualize the body of Christ as that one man, all of one mind and accord. All of them, individual parts of power and authority speaking in unity. Thy Kingdom come, thy will be done power being spread across the Earth all at once. Can you see how Satan crippled the early church by dividing them?

You know your assignment, My son. Show them the power of unity and show them the way to give their wills to Me. I have shown you the way to do this, My son, and I will reveal to you a more detailed map of how to reach the Kingdom. The secret is one to a few and then to many. When two or more are gathered, I am there also.

Everyone has his own responsibilities. But everyone has a moment or a few moments of time throughout each day. And let this be My silent army telling no one. Pray silently. At this time, My people are not to bow their heads or even close their eyes in public. I know everything they think and everything about them. I only want them to trust Me by turning their hearts to Me and silently repeating the Lord's prayer in their minds on a regular basis every day. This is not a command and there is no guilt of deciding not to do this or forgetting or being unable to for some reason. It will be a silent process where the cream will rise to the top. You are not to ask for any tithes or offerings. You can, however, accept gifts or donations to prepare teaching material.

The evening prayer before going to bed in their own homes should include bread and wine as we become bone of bone and flesh of flesh through the remembrance of the Lamb of God, the Lamb of the tribe of Judah. The other thing is training My people to undertake a part of the silent witness program—to pray for the events of the day, including the figurative dropping of a card of thanks to Me, your Lord Jesus. I desire and cherish the praises of My people. My Spirit dwelleth in the praises of My people. Let them understand that I am in control of everything about them and know the best solutions.

Bring their requests to Me in praise, because I will solve your problems at the same speed you turn your will to My will concerning your request. The perfecting of the saints will occur as a wave of My Spirit sweeps the ground. The Earth will shake and will tremor in pain. That will result in strict obedience to My Word for many. Others will fight the nudging of My Spirit, but it will be of no avail. They will not be able to resist the love and passion of My people at this time of crisis. They will see the one who delivers and passes over as the King of kings and the Lord of lords. The one once rejected is now the one saving them.

The world has waxed wonders, but I have not chosen the ways of the world for My people. They have chosen the men of renown as heroes and most admired. I am admired by those of ill-repute more than I am among the wealthy and the rich. I have my treasures also, and they are found most among the meek and the poor. You have chosen the ways of My treasures, and you have received much. You have invested your talents well. Now is the time of the revealing of the hidden treasures of darkness. There will be much quivering and the gnashing of teeth. You have heard the saying of My people that goes like this: *The gnashing of teeth is the rest for the wicked, and the joy of the Lord is the reward of the righteous.* I have made you righteous, and you are seeing the rewards of it now.

The home of the righteous is peace and quiet. You have seen quietness, and it will continue for a while as I continue to make the program more clear to you. You have traveled a rough road, but it is clear now to be at rest and in peace as you receive My words. The way has been made for you to move on a moment's notice. I have prepared the way for the time at hand. You will be traveling to the North Country soon. The work of the Branch has produced a special mark of acceptance to those in the north countries. Yea, I have risen and I will guide by historic markers.

January 9, 2000

The hope and the glory of the nations are about to come forth. The hope of the nations is the manifestation of the Prince of Peace. You are that hope for them. You represent the symbol of poverty. You are now weak and defeated in their eyes, but I will raise you up as a symbol of prosperity, physically as well as spiritually. The world will see the glory of the nations of God. They will flock to the glory land. You have given thought to the details of how I might do this. I have decided to encourage the people of My planting by inviting them to participate in a free-for-all battle of confidence.

You have been waiting, My son, and you are longing for this to happen in your lifetime. The waiting has ended, and the restoration begins today. You have begun the road to recovery. The individual wealth of each nation will flow. Both into Egypt and Samaria will the wealth flow as My people receive the wealth of the Moslem world as well. The Middle East will become the melting pot of the wealth of the Kingdom. Egypt and Syria will be as gateways into the Kingdom. The royal highway will run to the Capital from both Syria and Egypt.

You have been selected to teach My people the commandment of God to prosper and multiply. The average will be as the elite in My Kingdom. The average man will have prosperity beyond belief. The acres of diamonds will be a byword in describing My people. This prosperity has begun for you. You just haven't seen the evidence of what is here for you already. Prosperity builds prosperity, and you will see it grow as it moves across the land of My Kingdom. Believers will even be amazed at the speed in which I move as the harvester overtakes the planter. The world has long waited for such a time as this.

The prosperity of the wealthiest will be distributed among the poor in My Kingdom. The wealthiest will be the givers of wealth. The hoarders and empire builders will vanish as they see that the river has to continually flow and no dam can be built to stop or store.

The flow must continue to irrigate the crops of the givers. The seed planted grows quickly, and everyone will know that by continually giving they will continually receive. The wheel of prosperity will be one of perpetual motion—like the waters of the Everglades nourishing a forest forever. The water is always in abundance. Such abundance they cannot give away. Any obstruction will be taken away by the flood. Yes, you are a new man, My son. And you have been given the anointing to break the yoke of bondage upon My people. The work has begun, and the words are flowing. The power of the written word will amaze you.

The twentieth century was problematic in comparison to the prosperity of the twenty-first century. The work of building the swords of the last century will be turned to building plowshares this century. You have been given the script for this performance, and the blueprints have been laid before you.

The management of My Kingdom will be from My

perspective. And My seven eyes will see everything in the wheel of motion. The wheels will turn and turn, never stopping, and their appearance will be as if there is a wheel within a wheel full of eyes.

The words of wondrous things are beginning to reveal their meanings. The stars are all eyes of the universe, looking to planet Earth. The watchmen on the wall are waiting for the return of all that was stolen. The codes of understanding are being broken. The genetics of the Earth are being revealed in every living organism. The genetic engineering of the Earth is the secret to be revealed that contains the genes of all life. The engineering of the genetics of planet Earth are for the remission of all forms of death upon the Earth. And it will bring forth life abundantly.

The genes of the Earth are spiritual, and they will discover that the spiritual blood needs to be applied to the cause of death—the blood of the Lamb of God for the remission of all sin. All the costs of health preservation, if spent on making people understand the power of the blood, would complete all genetic research for eternity.

You, the *spiritual man*, have prospered. You have the keys to the doors of the Kingdom, and now you are to open them and let everyone enter. The way will be made clean and the red carpet laid out, the royal bloodstained carpet of the Kingdom. The blood of the Lamb will be applied outside the doors before the pass key will be given to them. The royal maitre d' of the Kingdom will usher everyone to the front desk, where they will receive a map of the

Kingdom. On this map they will see the way into the King's chambers with all His glory that He has received of His people.

The wheel of glory will turn, the wheel turning within the wheel. The inner sanctuary of the Kingdom will spin out blessings. The glory of light will shine through the clear and transparent body of that perfect man entering the Kingdom. The spirit of energy, the pure light will electrify the precious stones, the jewels and gems of the precious man. Crowns will be given, and a great veil will be brought forth.

The woman will enter. And they will see the glory of the man revealed in the woman, and they will see the glory of the woman revealed in the man. Both the son of man and the daughter of man are as one. The revelation of the man-child being born of the woman, the bride. The marriage supper of the Lamb is the giving and partaking of My Spirit. And the gathering at the supper will be the gathering of My people into unity before entering the house of the groom and His Kingdom.

My son, you have been chosen, and I will supply your need. Your need is not of this world. Your need is the understanding of My work, and the power and the authority for the anointing of My Spirit I have put upon you. The wonderful events of the future will be supplied by Me and My Spirit of Judgment. The Judgment still passes over My people. The blood on the mantle, when applied, covers the entire body, head, shoulders, and feet. The death angel will again pass over when he sees the blood. The judgment was the blessing that freed My people and destroyed the power of their persecutors in Egypt.

Again, the judgment will free My people and destroy the power of all persecutors. The end of time has not come and will never come for My people. They will flow into eternity as natural as waking up to a new day. That day will be a glorious day, beyond measure, when I glorify My people.

Time will never end, either; for the new ones I have not yet revealed. The new ones are the planting of My seeds upon the Earth that have not yet taken root. They will be revealed as the new generation of new believers taken out of the tribulation period of My trumpet judgments. Many will turn to Me, and every knee shall bow and confess Me as Lord of lords and King of kings in My presence.

There is a wave of knowledge that continually passes through My people that they are not yet able to grasp. The knowledge of the Kingdom will be revealed upon the tracks of the spiritual train that carries the good news of the Kingdom. This is the spiritual track that I traveled upon while I was on Earth. The wave of knowledge from My Father is available to you also. The understanding comes by not knowing in your mind all the other spiritual channels of misinformation placed upon you.

The misinformation highway is traveled by the spirits of anger, hate, immorality, and every other spirit of evil. This is easily tapped into as this misinformation is forced into My people's thoughts and dreams to quench out the spirit of righteousness. The tide has turned, and the spirit of righteousness prevails as My people do battle spiritually to free their minds to see the pure flow of the Holy Spirit of truth. The comforter that I sent is now available to travel the super highway of truth as it continually flows through the thoughts of My people. The comforter will not pass through evil accesses to My people.

A clear path must be forced into the minds of those lost in the robes of evil that covers their minds. My people do this through obedience, prayer, and spiritual battle. The way has now been made clear, My son, for you to travel upon this super highway of righteousness. Truth has prevailed, and you have blocked all the ways of evil and the world by totally eliminating your self-will. You have cast all your future hopes and dreams upon Me. You no longer have any hopes or dreams of this world.

You have set your sites upon the Kingdom, and you are ready.

The envelope of opportunity has reached the Kingdom for this generation. You are the first to enter into the Kingdom entrance of power and authority I have for My people. The dying of self is a long hard drive that you have navigated boldly. In your communications with others about the matters of this world, you wonder whether people may think you have lost all semblance of reality. If they only knew the truth of what you have found, they would then be seeking your help to find it for themselves. I am going to help the others by showing them the evidence of this truth.

You will demonstrate the power of the Kingdom's march to victory. I will show the world through your demonstration of power over the forces of evil. Did I not tell Daniel that those who know their God will do great exploits? The anger of the Lord has prevailed to judge My people in righteousness. The righteousness of My people, My Branch, will pass judgment upon the enemies of My people.

The uniting of the Kingdom has begun. My people of both Judah and Israel are aware and are awaiting the events of the future. They will still be surprised. They will recognize these events as the fulfilling of My Word. The balances have become even and level for the merging of My people. The time is now ready. The stuff is the occurrence of the events that will draw them together. There will be a great shaking going on, but it won't be dancing. It will be the delivering of My people out of bonds, and you will prevail over the forces of darkness.

You have withstood the test of time, and you will prevail. The time has become imminent, and you shall prevail. I have begun the countdown for the beginning of the ending of all bars and bonds that hold My people from being what they truly want to be—true sons of God, victors and overcomers. This will be a spiritual battle and victory: not by might, nor by power, but by My Spirit. You will deliver the message of encouragement to My people in the way that I tell you. You have given thought to the details of how I might do this.

I will conduct this with outstretched hands to My

people, inviting them to participate in the greatest manhunt ever held. Every man of God will rise up and follow Me. Free from all bondages of fear and doubt. You will be delivered to My people in an attitude of thankfulness and praise as they see whom I have selected to go before them. Michael will execute the judgment in your presence and the presence of the entire world. You will not be standing alone. I will have My prayer warriors with you in abundance.

You have seen the red ring around the sun as the rays shined upon your closed eyes. From between the leaves and branches of a green tree, the colors became magnificent florescent shades of the color scale surrounded by the orange ring. This signifies the beginning of a development I have described to you.

You will see the day begin soon when you see hoards of people wanting to know information I have given you. My people have seen My Word, but they have not heard the correct understanding of My Word. They are now coming to you to hear the understanding of My Word.

You will see the emergence of many who have fallen away but want to come back to a truth they can see, believe, and be a part of. Truth prevails. And you have introduced the truth of My Word, so that it can be easily understood.

*   *   *

The independent insurance companies are borrowing from the big banks to cover their losses from catastrophes coming upon the Earth. The way will soon be made clear to understand the words of the righteous King, the Holy One of Israel. They will want information on how to invest to cover their losses. The coming Kingdom is the answer to their problems. The avenue of hope and promise is the way leading to the Kingdom. They will be able to invest in the lives of those making the journey to get their best return. The joint venture between the avenue of hope will insure a most handsome return to investors.

It is written: "Seek ye first the Kingdom of Heaven and all these things will be added. I will never go back on My Word." This is the most secure investment of the twenty-first century. I guarantee a ten-fold return to My investors in joy and in peace.

The words have been spoken, and I have proclaimed the Word of the Lord unto My people. Now you will deliver the message of endearment—the message of understanding to My people of the closed book that has been opened up unto you. You will see the hope and the glory of the nations fall upon people as they are looked up to and are given the power and the authority to govern in the way that I lead. The trappings and the assets of My people will flourish as I ascend upon the glory of the nations. They will give to My people to gain mercy for what they have done to My people.

The business practices of taking and not giving will no longer work. The agony of giving will have to be overcome to succeed. Many will fail, but some will still prosper because of their giving freely and receiving. My Word is the truth. He who seeks to save his life will lose it, and he who gives it away will find it.

Many of the events of the future will rest upon your shoulders. The words that you speak will be believed and people will act accordingly. I will manage the Earth in a way that correlates to the words you speak. Did not I say "Command ye the Lord and I will reveal the truth that is to come"? You will be one fulfilling My Word. The world will turn and receive a windfall of blessings when they fall upon the truth of My Word.

After the blood and the pain of change, there will be great joy and harmony. The blessings will soar as the wind, and blessings will fall as the latter rain. I have gone forth, and I have given you My words of wisdom and council. The gifts of the seven spirits of the Lord have been activated into your life.

Now you will never be the same. The Word has changed you. The Word is also true of the Branch that you have borne on your shoulders into maturity. The tree of life has sprung into being a part of My Branch. You will see the meaning as we proceed.

The anguish and the pain you have borne are now over. The righteous Branch has framed itself into a living organism among My people. You have become the king of My domain that you have called the International Branch of the Lion of Judah. You will be looked to for leadership and knowledge of how to proceed. The council of My people will be dependent upon the council I give to you in our private moments.

The Word of Heaven is being spread out among My

people. The joint venture is happening between Heaven and Earth. The near death experiences have enabled My people in Heaven to participate with those upon the Earth. The knowledge is being transported by those who have visited the Homeland. An age is ending, and another is beginning. This is My home stretch, and the end will be victory circle. The Earth is in a victory circle, and it will be crowned with My people, My Heavenly city, Jerusalem. This will occur at the end and the beginning of another millennium.

* * *

You have been speaking to Me of many things. I have answered many questions about your hopes and dreams. But there is another about your family in Heaven. They are all excited about you. A little secret is that *everyone* in Heaven is part of your family. All of us here are one big family.

Your loved ones on Earth are given to you as part of the Heavenly family. We all know each other intimately except while on Earth where we all suffer a memory loss. Yes, even I had that lost memory of the glory of Heaven while upon the Earth. The advent of Christianity brought forth a new birth of heavenly beings—the birth of spiritual beings taken from the Word. They will all go through the process of self-determination, deciding on self-will or My will.

When this universe is fully redeemed, we will begin our next expansion plan. All My people will participate. We are a growing, big, happy family. The word of knowledge of yet undiscovered things has been given you. You have knowledge to dig deep into the universe of the unknown. The flying saucers are made of material that I have laid away in My universe. The universe has made its own self-expanding plan. The neurons of time have expansion capabilities similar to the stretching of a rubber band. Everything expands and moves and grows while the time band stretches forever. Nothing within the band dies or ages, yet it is free to move in order to govern in the way that I lead.

The undefined matter of existence will be made public to My people. The play on words is necessary to make My point and give you an understanding of things indescribable by words only. It takes the spiritual knowledge—the wonderment of the love, joy, and peace— always increasing at a steady rate, always changing, never growing old, always expanding.

Agape love, agape joy, agape peace.

The world will not know the atmosphere of My people in Kingdom life.

The Word has gone forth, and you will receive the offerings of My people in the form of products to be distributed in your behalf as an income for your words. The products will be your writings in the form of several books—*Thy Kingdom Come* series of books.

You were an abandoned child, so you were nourished to maturity alone without the care of the mother. But you have overcome. The work of being an overcomer and bringing unity to My church is to use an outcast not recognized and not under any influence of others.

January 10, 2000

If you have chosen Me and I have chosen you, is there not anything that we cannot do and accomplish? Yea, I say unto you that many will be sold into slavery of sin. But we will set them free by giving them the choice to be free. The Word is freedom to be free.

Tell them to gather all their problems as they would rake up grass into a basket and burn the grass. I tell them to cast their burdens upon Me; for My burden is light. Burdens are not of Me. Like the grass, the burdens are cast by My angels into the fire of hell and damnation. The Word has gone forth, My son, and you have been chosen to see the dawning of a new generation being born into the Spirit. The generation of evolutionary understanding is like a machine of many circles—an endless number of circles. There is a circle for everything, no matter how deep, how big, or how small your vision takes you. There is always a circle.

Now visualize a spiritual dial where every circle is registered similar to a mileage meter. Every circle has its DNA of everything, future and past, throughout eternity. Any information can be brought up. All you need to have is the code.

I am the Word, and the Word is the code. The secret to the code is abiding in Me. Ask whatever you will, and it will be done unto you. Through these teaching illustrations, My people learn about the Word of God in much the same way that a mechanic looks at a machine. All the information in this machine, that you may call God's computer, is free to My people. Seek ye first the Kingdom, and all of those things will be added.

*   *   *

You have just prayed for every soul upon the Earth. You have made each prayer intimate to each individual's special need. Now a special work has begun—an Earth changing work. The Word has gone forth that will touch and do something in every life. *Prayer moves the hands of God.* My hands are being moved to cover the Earth.

You said, "Give the EARTH its daily bread, forgive the EARTH its debts, and lead the EARTH not into temptation, but deliver the EARTH from evil; for thine is the Kingdom and the honor of the EARTH forever." This prayer has sent My angels to many who have never had a personal prayer said in their behalf. You have mobilized many angels in a unit of one bolt of lightning that affects every person. Continue sending this shock everyday as part of your prayers.

With enough people in agreement, all of one accord, the electricity of My Spirit will flow in a steady stream. The lights in the hearts of men will be turned on and more prayer will make the light brighter. The brighter it gets, the more the Earth is enlightened. The darkness must leave, and only My Kingdom remains to begin a new age. It is not by any war or political movement that the Kingdom will come. It will only come through the unified prayer of

My people abiding in Me. Everything else is My responsibility.

The enemy will try to resist and fight. But My eyes upon the Earth, which is abiding in Me, will act in obedience to My will. And a battle will be won. This is a process that will happen many times over in the life of every member marching into the Kingdom. We must fight to take the Kingdom. The weapons are in My hand that can be used by those who know Me, knowing My will and abiding in Me. The intimate relationship of My Word in the hearts of men and women is that same feeling that people in love have for each other.

When one becomes born again, that love relationship begins very softly with no demands to keep any laws.

Yes, I see your words, My son. You have spoken appropriately. This is not of you, My son; this is of Me. You have asked Me this without knowing it. When you were praying, My Spirit was speaking in thoughts and words you were not aware of. The entire Kingdom will be beautiful, and My Branch will be glorious as I manifest Myself through him. I have chosen the ones embedded and abiding in Me, regardless of any outcome. You have been willing to be the least or the highest, according to My perfect will. I have chosen to put you among the highest who rule in My Kingdom. In My Kingdom there will be many chiefs. We have great and varied jobs to do.

The Kingdom is being run by My management team. All decisions will be made by executive order. You see, the individuals from the top to the bottom are handpicked by the director at large. The supreme power of My Kingdom is the Holy Spirit. My heavenly council is like the seven eyes upon one stone. The seven eyes counsel the signet ring of authority. This is My standard. The seven eyes are seven positions I will appoint. The seven Spirits of God represent My personality of power and authority that will rule throughout the Kingdom.

Yes, I will rule with a rod of authority through My standard throughout the Kingdom. The signet ring of authority will be the administrator of My authority within his range of authority. The entire Kingdom will be exactly the way I have chosen for it to be. Every block will be in its proper place. Yes, you have visualized the Spirit, the soul, and the body of man as being My Kingdom.

Now visualize the pyramid. I am the chief cornerstone. Sons of God—My angels and My people are *both* called sons of God. I have revealed a secret now forming in your mind. Who are the angels? They are you. When an angel moves in your behalf, you are moving that angel by thoughts that you are not aware of. The spiritual man is the angel of that man. There is a soul man as well. The soul man lives in the flesh now. My Spirit also dwells within the soul when I am asked to enter. The angels of men surround My throne and engineer the thoughts of the soul man under My direction. The soul man, in turn, looks to Me inwardly as I am speaking to you now. The inward man of Me dwelling within and the angel of your spirit become one.

When your spirit is one with My Spirit, your spirit is

omnipresent just as Mine is. The mind of man was made in that the larger portion is closed with locked doors. There is an awakening coming to My people where they will no longer want to remain as the caterpillar, but will want to be changed into a butterfly. This can and will happen to all those who truly give themselves to Me. How can anyone truly abide in Me as I abide in you without sharing My life as I share yours?

We are a Trinity: the Father, the Son, the Holy Spirit. I am all that the Father is, and the Father is all that I am. The Spirit is My Father and Me. The three are one. So the Spirit dwelling in you is the Trinity. The Father chose to give Me a Kingdom and made man in our image where We would dwell.

You could look at this as being a change of operational procedures taking place through the creation of mankind. You have independent thinking and desires. I have chosen to enjoy My Kingdom through the fulfillment of all the emotions of My people of varied shapes, ambitions, and personalities. The independence of mankind has been turned inward to Me to be a part of the Trinity. Now we become one. I am one with you, just as I am one with the Father.

How can I be one with you and also one with each of the other members of the body? When I have a will totally submitted and only desiring My will, I give him desires that harmonize like a beautiful song. Every note is in proper position to become a beautiful symphony of music. That will be the result of people giving Me their wills. No butterfly ever wants to return to being a worm. This is the secret of the Garden of Eden. The knowledge of good and evil was self-will that has gone the route of independent thinking and rejecting My Spirit of love.

The workmanship of the Kingdom will be performed similarly. Nothing will be magical. It will be more like a fine watch ticking exactly in the right moment for the perfect time. The events in the future, that will harmonize My people, will be the awakening that is to be occurring soon.

The relationships of My people will be harmonized to the others by the actions of the outside world from outer space. "The aliens have landed!" will be the cry of My people. "And what shall we do?" they will say. I will again manifest Myself as I engage the enemy of My people. I will be much appreciated at the time of the fly by.

The world will be confused. The angers will emerge from all directions, and My people will be confiscated to arrange for a bounty of My people in exchange for peace. The world will seem unprepared for what is about to take place, but I have made arrangements and My plan will succeed. The plan is to suspend the entire network of enterprise development upon Earth. This will be like the Tower of Babel in reverse.

All My people will speak one language again. The beginnings of the empire builders will become as if their development plans have been broken. The fanaticism of the people will be overwhelmed by the indwelling Spirit, and My people will enjoy the marvelous awakening of My

Spirit being shown in the practices of supernatural manifestations of My Spirit. They will see men as they have never seen them before. The world will be in wonderment of what is happening.

My overwhelming appearance will frighten many of My people, but the majority will be at peace with themselves as they see the manifestations of My power. The entire universe will be ablaze. The entire Earth will be as a dawning day of sunlight as I accelerate the rotation of the Earth. The evenings and the day will meet at midday. Time elapses in a mystical haze. The time machine has to run its course, but it does not need to be slow. The evening will fall in the afternoon. The timepieces will be accelerated to meet the day's beginning. The evenings will become overwhelmingly bright with excitement; and as My light shines on them, they will be changed in the twinkling of an eye; and they will know that the Kingdom is at hand.

You are to publish this on the mountain of My people in the land of Israel as Jerusalem becomes the wind-driven center of commerce. The energy given in the enlightenment of My people will enlarge the city overnight and will demand the commerce of the world for support.

The support will flow in as camel loads become trainloads, and trainloads become as bridges of commerce from the hub to the edges of the Earth as if it were a great big wheel. You are wondering about the Book of Revelation and the seven trumpet judgments. I have set the world up to be judged by My people.

The documents are correct, and they will occur as I

have said. But the beginning is not the end, nor is the end the beginning. The entire timeline has been developed in a way that it intercedes into becoming a circular event rather than a longitudinal line. The time of space occurs at a different rate. The entire universe rotates around a *Son* also. I am that Son, and the circle never ends. The Earth is somewhere within that circle.

What would happen if I decided to put time on hold? The Earth would not disappear. It would still be in the universe that rotates around the Son of man. The rotation of the Earth around the *sun* would end. The Kingdom is My dwelling place. So the Earth does become the center of the universe—the dwelling place of the Son.

*   *   *

You have been wondering about the Millennial Reign of Christ and the war of Armageddon. I said a day is as a thousand years, and a thousand years is as a day.

By now you are thinking I am full of surprises, and that is true. So let's say we put the millennium on hold as well as Armageddon.

You are asking about Satan being locked up for the thousand years and then being cast into the lake of fire. It will happen just as I said, when time begins again.

Satan is not put on hold; he is put on a refining mission of the other planets. His rebellion put the whole universe in chaos. The end becomes the beginning when I decide to arrange My Kingdom into what you call outer space.

We then begin a new Garden of Eden on each planet. Purification is with fire, and temptation is needed for My test. I don't want any more devils.

So the war that goes on upon the Earth is both the beginning and the ending of My universe. As I am the Alpha and the Omega dwelling upon the Earth, you are asking about Heaven. Heaven comes to Earth as the new Jerusalem, My bride in whom I dwell.

Everything I speak to you must be in strict accordance with My written Word, in truth and example of recorded events. Not one jot nor tittle will ever be changed. Check every word you have written, and it will be in perfect accordance. The difference is that I have given you new eyes to see and new ears to hear. Yes, My son, this is Holy Ground we have been walking upon. You are to keep this knowledge to spill out as you speak. Did not I say make your book spectacular? We will do that also. But there is a time to reveal and a time to withhold. You will bring out certain scriptures at unusual times that seem to fit unusually well.

*   *   *

The way has been made for you, My son. You will travel fast, and you will travel soon. The day has arrived now that I will let you see the future as no one has ever seen it before. You have unraveled the question box of My people—questions of high hopes and adventures of the future and the future of Kingdom living and life.

You have been advised in My Word that I have prepared a place for you in My Father's house, and that I have. My Father's address is planet Earth as you have seen in what I have revealed.

The putting together of the property of the Kingdom is by good works, and many mansions will be there. The other thing that I have prepared for My people is the outer portion of the soul of the Earth. This is a band like a ribbon that will appear in the clouds and circle the Earth. It will appear like the band around Jupiter.

This is My outer garment of the soul and is part of the management plan of My people. The urbanization of planet Earth will be upon this platform in space. It will be called *the ribbon of praise.* On this platform, there will be the musical choirs of Heaven. The sound waves will flourish and rotate in various tones and sounds the way sounds reverberates if you were inside a bell. The glorious musical sounds will go throughout the heavens. The penetration of My music will enslave the sound masters with the praises of My people throughout the universe.

The way will be made clear soon for My people to see the vision of their hopes and ambitions of the future. They will be impressed with My excellent architectural designs of My Kingdom. The wonderful nightlife of My people will never end. Intercourse will continue as we continue to deliver the seed of life onto the other planets.

The seed of Adam will prevail throughout the universe. There have been many other creations in the past in My perfecting process, but there was only one man created in our image, and His seed will keep flourishing forever in a population explosion throughout the universe.

In My Word, you see that the man and the woman will not be given in marriage, but they will be as the angels. The secret is that the angels are not given in marriage because they belong to Me. When a marriage takes place, a couple moves out of their father's house into a home of their own. I have said in My Father's house are many mansions. This is like one home for everyone. The supernatural understanding is that we will all enjoy each other's company as we trade the energies of ourselves with others.

In the Old Testament, My men, even My prophets, had many wives. This is the way that I intended it to be. The sin was not the many wives, it was Solomon's submission to the influences of his wives that he knew was his sin. Did I not say in My Word that seven women would encompass one man and My Branch would be glorious? Do I not say there will be a great marriage supper of the Lamb? Do I not indwell the lives of My people? Do I not enjoy the joys of My people? Is not sex a joy for My people?

Many people look upon sex as evil or bad. But I designed it as a joy and a blessing for My people. The birthing of children will be a new joy and comfort beyond measure. The mothers will be blessed abundantly as each new member is born into My Kingdom.

The glory of the nations will no longer be financial as silver and gold. But the glory will be the bloodlines of the Lamb of God being brought into purification through My divine plan of reproduction. The valleys of mourning will cease. The moods of My people will change. Impatience, nervousness, and anger will no longer exist.

The long awaited transfer of wealth of the nations to My people is coming soon. The day has arrived now that you have been taken by Me into My arms, and you will soon be seen as the Branch of My planting.

The man-child conceived by Me has been born upon your shoulders of patience, My son, allowing Me to do a work in My people in answer to your prayers. Your book is being closed for the moment. But I want you to print everything just as you have written.

This will be My message to My people for today, the day of Glory.

*　*　*

The ways have been made and the roads have been paved for your journey through the valleys and over the hills and across the seas of My Kingdom. The Earth is mine and I am taking it back now. Anger and frustration or righteous indignation some say are with Me also. How could I not indwell My people and not feel their pain? Righteous indignation does dwell within Me, and I will act up on it in restoring My people into their Kingdom, the Kingdom of our Prince of Peace, the Lord Jesus.

You have worn My presence; and in spite of some downfalls, you have regained My acceptance. By My people, by your faith and obedience in hard times, the reward has been with Me to see you through. I am well pleased by being of service to you. The banner of understanding is now being seen as an emblem of satisfaction to both of us.

Yes, My son, there is a connection between your prayer to give the Earth this day the *Earth's* daily bread and forgive the *Earth's* debts and lead the *Earth* not into temptation, but deliver the *Earth* from evil. Yes, the Earth can be delivered from evil. I only move at the command of My people through prayer.

When you abide in Me, My Holy Spirit directs your thoughts so that I command My people to command Me.

There is a great distance from being in command and being in control. I'm in control of all the Earth, and I am in command of those abiding in Me. This is like the slave who says, "I am in the command of My master." So when one abides in Me, I, like that slave, am in the command of My people abiding in Me. When people are not abiding in Me, I become in control. So when in command the Holy Spirit leads you as a son of God, an administrator. And I execute.

Now you can understand the importance of your prayer to deliver the Earth from evil. Your abiding and your prayers of deliverance have caused a change for the better of My deliverance plan of My people. The results of the upcoming events have gone from being critical to controlled optimism for full recovery.

Yes, My son, I would like to pray into existence a new thing, a new thing of dynamic qualities, a *Dynatetratonic equation,* or the diet that prevents aging. This will happen in an instant. The credibility of a move like this will be seen in the lives of many who believe and receive a reliable replacement of organs under the managed care of My people praying in the privacy of their bedrooms.

The one place of comfort and rest where we can communicate the best is in deep dreams and in deep prayers. This new technology of genetic non-aging remedies is now being designed for the world's richest people.

The purpose of My coming to you, My son, is for you to discourage the forces of evil from destroying My people by plagues and other engineered devices. I have begun the work of everlasting life by educating you in the profession of *giving* everlasting life as we resurrect and enlarge the lives of both men and women who are dead and the bedridden who are dying. The work will be the equivalent of the resurrection of your Lord and Savior, Jesus Christ of Nazareth. The truth about it is just calling upon the name of Jesus for the dynamic power of the resurrection.

The Dynatetratonic equation may be a new phrase in your vocabulary, but it is simply the knowledge that you have the power of such a prayer. It's just that simple. But getting that degree of belief has been the problem. The words of My healings are simply being spoken at the moment of the right faith level of that request. This also determines whether it is instantaneous or drawn-out healing.

The anguish of prayer is feeling that surge of doubt at the moment the healing or resurrection energy is released. The answer of that prayer of confidence can be answered by addressing another issue of faith: the support of My people being behind the prayer in unity, all of one accord.

What about Me or someone else who may be alone you ask? The answer is simply abiding. When you abide in Me, I am your prayer support. You know that you have given Me your will regardless of what may come. You now have the confidence of knowing that I am behind your belief system. IT IS MY FAITH THAT YOU CAN COUNT ON. Just as you are able to cast your burden upon Me, and your worries and frustrations disappear. You now have the ability to say, BY THE FAITH AND THE POWER OF THE LORD JESUS. I now say unto you, "Rise and walk, or come forth out of the grave." And it will be done according to your word abiding in Me.

You have been given the power and the authority of the blood of Jesus Christ in full measure. The ability to pray in the name of Jesus with power and the authority of the blood is dynamic power beyond your belief. The power, majestic in the name of Jesus, is the highest order of all authority. The blood of the Lord Jesus is the power of the ever-cleansing or washing away of sin. The power and the authority of the name of Jesus, My Son, are the name and power of all names. The power and the authority of the blood are a cleansing authority that reveals Jesus Christ within the power of the one speaking. This understanding knows that in the power of the blood of Jesus Christ, your countenance is washed with blood and the fleshly man is washed away in the spiritual. So the spiritual forces, both good and evil, see My Son, Jesus, in your countenance.

So when you speak these words by the power and the blood of Jesus Christ, the enemy *sees* Jesus Christ working within you in all of His power and authority abiding in you. You go with Christ Jesus with His full power and authority. Because Jesus has made you one with Himself as He is one with Me the Father, we are all one—the Dynatetronic equation or energy of the highest equation— I the Father, Jesus the Son, the Holy Spirit, and you.

Go forth as one of My sons. You are *all* of the sons and daughters of God.

Yes, there is something else coming upon you, My son. An Eagle will rest upon your shoulder. This will be visible only through spiritual eyes. The anointing of the Branch will be in the form of an Eagle. The yoke is taken off your shoulder with the anointing of the Holy Spirit of authority, the Eagle. I have gone from Lamb to a Lion, and My Spirit from Dove to Eagle. Dynatetronic: energy of the highest equation dwelling and abiding together as one.

January 12, 2000

The less effort will bring the greatest return. The giving of self involves the less effort. The easier you look at this, the easier it becomes. It is another walk of easy steps that begins with the first step: one simple prayer, the Lord's prayer. For the answer of a problem made by this simple prayer request, one can always rest. Rest assured that the problem is taken care of, and it will work itself out the best possible way.

A way that the enemy casts discouragement upon My people is that he tells them to keep their eyes on the problem, looking at each progress to see if the Lord is doing what He says He will do. Any seed of doubt may hinder, delay, or even stop the work that I have already put in motion for the perfect solution.

When an irregular heartbeat of faith occurs, a spiritual problem then occurs. Like you see when there is a problem in a computer network, they have to work around the problem. They must work around so the rest of the network is not contaminated. That's how I work. The breakdown can be avoided after the prayer is made, then refuse to focus on the problem.

Whenever the situation in progress enters your mind, let that be a mental reminder to thank and praise Me for what I am doing. And set your mind to doing My will in another new area of your life. When Satan attaches and people put demands for payment on whatever it may be, your response should be: "I have given this the highest priority, and the solution is being worked on. The answer will be coming soon, and I will be letting you know." The faith of My people will uncover the hidden treasures of obedience to My Word.

The Word will perform, and the work will be accomplished. The least effort involves a giveaway program. Give Me your faith to work with, and never take it back with doubt of My faithfulness or ability to perform your command. This is the easiest way of using My command and control. It is to work at your command rather than to be in your control. One is positive; the other is negative.

The ability of the successful mergers to take place provides a way of taking the Kingdom without force. We will buy it with their own money, so to speak, similar to My people borrowing all the silver and the gold just as they were leaving town. I see the smile on your face as you see how I refer to Egypt being a system of the world. I will revolve in a circle of finances that will spin off blessings and assets to My chosen few who have been obedient to My Word.

Although he does not fully understand how, Bill Gates is a blessing for Me to be used in the palm of My hand. You tell him I know all the abuse that he has taken from those who fear his empire. He is a righteous man, and people fear him for this reason alone.

He is bewildered by his success and knows that it is not of his own doing or planning. He has submitted to My divine plan without a true understanding. The trust he puts in Me to make his decisions is a way of abiding his business in Me. The avenues of success are very simple if you know where the road goes and where it ends. Bill knows where the road goes and where it ends. He's looking for an exit to find a rest spot to unload the indigestion he is feeling in his stomach.

You will see him soon, and I want you to review an exit plan that will give him the rest that he greatly desires. The sign is just ahead, and he needs to start slowing down. The remedial processes of memory are becoming more sophisticated, and he needs to know the route of intercourse onto the highway of new understanding.

The understatement has been made that a bad step will result in a collision of international proportions by injecting the element of distrust in the system.

The objectives will be to interject the social aspects with the spiritual possibilities being introduced into various contingency plans. The decisions will be made in an appropriate way at the appropriate time. Bill has had dreams of you also, but doesn't know who you are. He is expecting you soon, and the real test will come when I introduce the two of you. Will the test light up the city, the state, or the world? The world will be enlightened.

I am telling you now of something more important to the world than the internet. The next challenge will be to unravel the questions the world is asking about having the ability to communicate the problems and solutions in a way that the world will respond to a one-world government, but not one of their own making.

The trial and error process will no longer work. The divine plan of salvation needs a surge of enlightenment to enter the next step into the Kingdom of God here on Earth. The access code is through the blood of the Lamb of God, sacrificed on Calvary for the remission of the sins of the world.

The coming Kingdom of God is here. We are entering into the Kingdom one step at a time. The reverse of creation started one step at a time towards death after the seed of sin was planted by disobedience. The beginnings and the endings evolve the same way, only in opposite directions.

The seed of righteousness was planted by your obedience many years ago, and we are proceeding one step at a time back to the tree of life found within the Kingdom of God.

The wages of sin are death, and the gift of God is eternal life. The life of the Father in the Son, and the life of the Son are His body of believers. The arrangement is for the benefit of all mankind.

The bloodline of life eternal lies within the blood line. It is either your blood or My blood. Your choice: one leads to death and one leads to life. The true life is in the blood of the Lamb of God.

In the end was the beginning, and in the beginning was the end. Both decided by a decision of the will, and it is either self-will or My will, either the will of the way of life or the will of the way of death. One can choose selfishly or abundantly. The way we have chosen is abundantly, and abundantly we will travel.

You will be constantly giving away everything you have to the amazement of your family and friends. But they will see the flow of the blood also—the flow of the love you have for those in need.

You have been given the gift of prosperity by your giving, the giving of yourself to Me. I will not hold back. Everyone will say you have the keys to the vault, jokingly, because everyone will see that you have the key of a greater treasure than the vault. You have discovered the keys to the Kingdom.

Abiding in all the glory, the power, and all the authority of the blood of the Lamb in Christ Jesus, yea, I say unto you, "The world has never seen such glory poured upon anyone as they see that I pour out." All glory, power, and wealth are Mine to give as I please.

My son, be not concerned of what to say or not to say to anyone. Rest assured that by only desiring My will allows us to have such a close relationship that wisdom, council, and other gifts are free to work in a way of timing that your thought pattern is according to My Father's time piece, making your presence always perfect.

This can be done if there is no unconfessed sin in your life, and all your future self desires and will have been given to Me. Never feel that you arrived too late, or I should not have done that. As long as you abide in Me, all time and events are the way I have designed them. Look for My appearance or manifestation in the strange, unusual, or rare event.

You have been spoken about to Me by My Son. He has

given Himself to the joy of being with you. You have become the joy of His heart, and you have received a fellowship degree of My honor for being an abiding cosmonaut of inner space.

The space war has not been one of outer space, but of inner space, the space of abiding between Jesus My Son, and Me the Father, the inner circle of the Holy of Holies. That is where you are dwelling at this time and will dwell throughout the end of time: in the inner circles of our heart. Now as you abide with us, we are all of one mind and accord.

*   *   *

The plan of environmental control has new meaning when applied to the Kingdom of God. To wake up the people and send out the message of the Kingdom is our aim, and the religiously correct methods are being interfered with. So let's try a new approach.

The underworld of crime has free access to all of those who need to be changed the most into the image of God. We have something the crime networks of the world want and that is access to the information of power. We can work a plan that will work marvels for them and our Kingdom as well.

Bill Gates is known as the keeper of the gate of information with his new discoveries. The software he is making will be his method of exposing it.

The idea is to conceive a plan that will enable the people

a way of environmental weather control. The method is easy to be understood by everyone knowing the secrets of life's intelligence. The network will expose those secrets in a new way that can easily be understood by adding an element of surprise into the information that men and women already obtained through experiencing marriage.

The secrets of a good marriage are for each one to know the needs of their partner and to fill that need. The same is true with the environment. Love is the seed of faith in any relationship, and the need of the environment can be filled with the element of love, one for another.

The thinking can be changed in a very subtle way. We change the environment by the way we act toward each other. If it were known that we are all parts of the same person, we would take care of all sores and scratches on the body. The same is true with the environment. Some know and understand this, but they need to be motivated.

The motivation will come from the information about the upcoming events that are ready to happen on planet Earth. The world system and the planet itself will be changed dramatically for good. You have been waiting and watching for things to change.

The change is coming, but it is coming in a way you never dreamed of. My power and authority will be invested in you in a way you do understand in the gift of giving oneself to Me. This is the gift of free life as well as eternal life. The freedom for one to be himself, but free from the effects of selfishness. Then all problems one has are Mine and My sole responsibility.

This power and authority you are now receiving is the power and authority to truly love others as yourself, knowing that all are one in My sight. Love multiplies in numbers, and love has power to supply the needs of all types.

Maybe we should call this Bill Gates' love machine. Sometimes he doesn't feel loved by the world. But the world will become love in that I will build the energy of love into the world economic systems. This will begin in a way that seems strange to human beings, but works in the mindset of building My empire of the Kingdom of God on Earth as it is in Heaven. The evening lovefest of My people will be the intercession of filling the needs of others that will become like a force of perpetual motion.

The ideas to put this in motion are in the mind you are abiding in, and I will explain it now to you. The new beginnings will occur in the event that is coming, the event of circular motion in the environment that will endanger the lives of everyone as the Earth shifts.

You will see this in action soon. It will not seem too bad until the levels of the sun increase. The ice caps melt because the poles change, and the ice becomes placed in a warmer atmosphere. This is a slow-moving total disaster coming upon the Earth that everyone sees clearly. The mountains will seem like a refuge and will become heavily populated.

The only solution will be the plan we introduce to the world through Bill Gates' software. The Earth will be burning from heat, and the ice will be melting rapidly.

Within a few days of the event, the world will be ready to listen to anyone who offers any hope.

I will appear to you in that offer of hope. Bill Gates will have an opportunity to offer the hope to the world. We will decide to become a little more revealing as we decide to remove the forces of evil through evaporation. The heat will evaporate the water into a cloud, and it will form an Earth shield that we will enlarge to become a ledge of matter lighter than air, like foam. The bubbles will enlarge and freeze in the outer atmosphere.

This will become the opportunity for the future of mankind. The idea is for Bill Gates to develop a software of aggregate molecules. What I mean by this is the establishment of a few molecules of fiber to be formed in a variety of ways to be made into air to breath. They will be taken in as food, and the body will convert this to gas in the stomach that can be breathed through the lungs. The idea is a way to establish breathing for outer space.

This will enable the population to move to the outer shelf of planet Earth. This is the urbanization of planet Earth and the development plan of the future. The software is a key because it involves a silicone solution made in extreme heat that Bill understands as far as making software tablets that disappear when the energy from a computer engages in the operation of mailing documents.

This product will be manufactured on Earth and transferred through space on a computer system known as the *transfiguration system* into space. This will open many avenues of enlightenment. The enlightenment of these discoveries are not by power. It is only in the reality of the abiding in Me that you find this pure spirit of knowledge.

*   *   *

The son of perdition, the anti-christ, asked if he could be sent down upon the Earth. My response was no, not at this time. The Kingdoms of God have become the Earth's, as well as the kingdom of this Earth have become the Kingdom of God and His Son, Jesus Christ. I have spoken it. All the power and all the glory belong to Me, and I am giving the glory to My people.

You will see this on the news if you look closely. You have been chosen, My son, to be a servant of My people. You have not been chosen alone. There are many that fill that office.

The words have been spoken, and the ends of time are turning to Me for direction. The beginning and the end are waiting to see what my command is. The time loop will be straightened, and they will be able to see soon that the end of time is not near.

There is another bend now that was not seen before, and the time belt is extended as we straighten out the bend. These are times that My understanding turns in a way that you could not. There are many secrets in the words of My prophets that they did not know or understand to be within the words that were being spoken.

You are again wondering. You are asking, "Am I being

deceived? Does this really line up with the Word of God?"

The answer is that you will see as you wait upon Me. Keep the words sealed from others as we see this through together as you abide in Me and My Word. The Word has been spoken and will not be retracted; the meanings only need to be revealed by you, My son. The words are spoken, and the words are true. The words have been shown to the wind to be scattered among My people in the mouths of two or more witnesses, and My Word will be confirmed.

I have chosen more than two to confirm your word. You will see them in wonder and amazement as they reveal themselves soon. You have been speaking the words of truth and of life, and all will know that I have spoken through you, My son.

My servant has been sent, and I will follow. He speaks the word, and I perform his spoken word. You have seen it in the past, and you will see it again and again. My Word will never grow old. It is always a new fresh word to My people with understanding that My Word has neither beginning nor end, and the options are endless as revelation builds upon revelation. You have only broken the surface of My Word.

The words of a sailor are *Bon Voyage, have a good trip*. My words to you, My son, are that we will have many good voyages as we sail from Genesis to Revelation and from Revelation to Genesis. We will be looking at the beauty of creation that has never before been seen in My Word. There is also a beauty of light in darkness that has not been seen before.

The journey will always be a pleasant journey as we discover throughout the Kingdom of My Word here on Earth.

The Ivory Coast is the way that I would describe something that you will be developing soon. It will be the development of a new product you will call Ivory Coast, an anti-aging product for My people. It will be a pure product with a simple formula, a formula that anyone can make or develop in their own home.

It involves the intake of food in the same product that would be sent to those in outer space. With a pure product, there is no bowel movement or even a need for a urinary tract in your body. You will simply diet on My new product.

Decimal, meaning ten other, is the ten other products of natural energy. They are [1] Sun [2] Rain [3] Wind [4] Magnetism [5] Steam [6] Heat [7] Natural growth [8] Earth motion [9] Moving water, and the most basic of all [10] Birth. We are putting all this energy into a single product in a very clever way.

The ideal welding of these energies together is the birth of all energy in the new birth of Jesus Christ, who is all energy. He is the energetic one running and controlling the universe. The formula is birthing the product in the Spiritual Realm and then delivering it to the physical realm, where it can be used and consumed through eating.

The communion service is an example of what I am describing to you. I took the stripes upon My flesh and shed My blood for My people. The energy in the physical sacrifice provides energy in the Spiritual Realm to heal and to save.

A *symbol* would represent each one of these energies in the form of two letters. For example: Sn=Sun, Rn=Rain, Wd=Wind, Mg=Magnetism, Em=Earth Motion, and Bi=Birth. The word used to describe the symbols is the same as the one used to define the products of natural energy: *Decimal.*

So now we have symbols of all the natural energies upon the Earth refined to one little capsule. This is the capsule for ending aging and restoring your flesh to a new beginning with each capsule taken.

This is the capsule of the tree of life and leads everyone to the Ivory Coast of Paradise. It must be taken both into our spirit and our body of flesh each day. This is both the spiritual and physical that activates the faith for this renewed physical life.

Pray this at the end of the Lord's prayer everyday at your daily communion of wine and bread. End by praying the Lord's prayer and eating some type of fruit symbolizing the fruit of the tree of life: "I now take in the DECIMAL and fruit of the tree of life."

This will be the beginning of the physical life beginning. The indwelling spirit is the core of the universe where the seed of the life of the creator dwells. This is not the maker of life, but the creator of new life. The indwelling spirit's life is by the two coming together to create new life, and this is the birthing process of My man-child.

So the indwelling spirit is your spirit submitting to the Spirit of the Trinity to indwell the personality of the Son and let Him possess your life as His own. The spiritual battle is a battle for possession of the soul. Some of My people let the Holy Spirit and their spirit be one, but won't give up possession of their soul.

Therefore, one who is spiritually reborn who has refused to submit to My will is the subject of a contest for possession of the soul. When rebellion against doing My will occurs, that one becomes a candidate for doing Satan's will. If the soul separates totally from the indwelling Holy Spirit, the soul submits to Satan, and Satan indwells the soul and takes possession. My Holy Spirit, although still indwelling the heart or spirit, has no more influence until the soul is delivered.

The spiritual battle is a battle to gain territory to set up military operations, spiritually, and the battle grounds are the souls of men. The wars upon Earth are never against people. Satan possesses the souls of My people to destroy them before they become born into My Kingdom. When Satan gets his possessed people fighting in wars, then he is in a position to destroy the righteous who are forced to join the battle.

The wages of sin are death, and Satan always wants to pay in full.

This is the day that I have chosen for you, My son, to show you the inverted wheel within the wheel. This is the holiest work of all, the work of listening unto My voice and being obedient to it.

You are right when you say the inner wheel within the wheel determines the work of the entire wheel all full of eyes. The inner wheel is the one wheel of which the entire work of the entire wheel rests. They are the architects who care to and structure the goals, and determine the ways and means of obtaining these objectives.

The outer wheel is all the assemblies of worship that want to be obedient and are seeking My perfect will. I have an assembly of a few or many to work with who are waiting for a word from Me to submit to and to be obedient to.

The inner circle is the pastors they look up to for guidance, the ones they look to whom they trust to know Me and hear My voice. They don't believe there is any other way than finding and following a pastor or leader who hears My voice.

The answers they seek may be served on a network approach over the internet. Draw out the large wheel full of eyes in your mind. The little wheel or the wheel within the wheel is a smaller wheel, but a stronger wheel.

The key of understanding is to understand the logic of leverage. Rather than wheels, if they were straight bars, visualize them as levers or pry sticks. The power of each lever is determined by where the axis is placed to pry upon. The closer the axis is placed to the object to move, the more power one has in using the lever. I move the axis to be sure we always have the most result for the least amount of work. This is My specialty, and no motion is wasted because I also know exactly how fast and how far the object needs to be moved.

How is a pastor to know what needs to be moved, let alone how fast or how far it should be moved? Many pastors today look to see what others have done. They ask questions, hold staff conferences, and then make a decision. These decisions include church officers, building projects, study groups, and teachers.

They rate their success by their increase in membership, and each week they count and post the number of those who ask Me into their hearts. They pray for Me to bless their work and ask their members to pray for revival and for money to buy a new bus. This is how My people work for Me; they work very hard and are loyal and dedicated to their work.

The embassies of many governments work the same way in foreign countries by watching and seeing what the other government or agency is doing. This is a problem for My people. Almost every church teaches the same gospel, the same Sunday School classes. But they have different names and labels. They have not been able to grasp the principle of leverage.

Now visualize the wheels as a network of various churches all teaching the basic doctrines of salvation, by grace, and the other main points of agreement. What if we were to establish city, county, and neighborhood communication centers for pastors and church leaders by their own choice to participate in prayer for each other? What if we have them pray over the internet in order to establish a test for everyone to see how the "plumbline principal" works?

This would allow us to introduce My method of being the head of the church.

To start the prophets would consist of seven selected pastors to be the eyes of a larger number of pastors. After this is shown and taught with a demonstration of My power, then I will be able to establish a line of communication of seven eyes upon one stone into the churches for each congregation: as with one to a family, then to a city, and to a nation; Abraham, Israel, and the world.

*   *   *

Yea, I have been with you, My son, and you have delivered the message as I intended. Your feelings have not interfered. Your emotion and your passion are to be admired by My people. You have won a spiritual battle. The Word has been sent out that you have conquered the enemy, and they are running for cover. You have divulged secrets of the Kingdom.

Yea, I have been present with you and also abiding in you. The various quotations were of Me as you spoke with a listening ear. You have been marvelous before the Kingdom of Heaven, and they are shouting for joy. The Kingdom is in great celebration of what you have revealed. You have revealed the early entry into the Kingdom tonight without knowing it.

You stated that the Kingdom of God may happen at the sixth seal before the seven trumpets and the rest of the seven bowl judgments of the tribulation. What a surprise it was when My people heard these words! They recognized My Word spoken through you and knew that it was true. I have spoken these words through you that you were not aware of. They have shocked both kingdoms:

Satan's kingdom with fear and the Kingdom of Heaven with joy.

You are asking, "How will I be able to tell the body of Christ?" The answer is—don't. Don't speak this to anyone. But write it out in your book, and I will put the pieces together for you.

My words have been spoken. They are truth, and they are life.

The Lord is my shepherd; I shall not want. He maketh me to lie down in green pastures: he leadeth me beside the still waters. He restoreth my soul: he leadeth me in the paths of righteousness for his name's sake. Yeah, though I walk through the valley of the shadow of death, I will fear no evil: for thou art with me; thy rod and thy staff they comfort me. Thou preparest a table before me in the presence of mine enemies: thou anointest my head with oil; my cup runneth over. Surely goodness and mercy shall follow me all the days of my life: and I will dwell in the house of the Lord for ever.

—Psalm 23

About the Illustrator

Pat Marvenko Smith began her career as an artist out of a sincere desire to serve the Lord and make His Word, the Bible, easier to understand. She began her Revelation series of prints in 1981 to supplement a Sunday School class she was teaching. She has completed 40 magnificent illustrations that represent the Book of Revelation. They are now available in art prints and visual teaching materials through her company, Revelation Productions. Her work is highly regarded throughout the U.S. and Canada in respect to its beauty, accuracy, and attention to detail. Pat brings with her artwork an educational background in fine and commercial arts. She implements the discipline and technique she has learned over the years into her unique illustrative style.

About the Author

Gary Larrabee has nurtured his love of God through His Word for more than 20 years. He believes the Lord has revealed to him revelation into the understanding of the new millennium. The Bible is relevant to every generation, and it is simply a matter of truly understanding what the Lord is saying that makes us overcomers. After hearing God's voice, Gary has learned the importance of listening to what God has to say. He is taking one step at a time and has discovered that if he endures to the end, God will always provide a way, or bridge, around every obstacle. He has lived and traveled around the world, and is currently residing in the Pacific Northwest.